THE
POWER OF AUTHORS

A RALLYING CRY FOR
TODAY'S WRITERS TO RECOGNIZE
THEIR POWER, RISE TO THEIR CALLING, AND
WRITE WITH MORAL CONVICTION

BY EVAN AND LOIS SWENSEN
Publishing with Power, Principle, Purpose, and Perspective

PUBLICATION CONSULTANTS
We Believe In The Power Of Authors

8370 Eleusis Drive, Anchorage, Alaska 99502-4630
books@publicationconsultants.com—www.publicationconsultants.com

ISBN Number: 978-1-59433-869-4
eBook ISBN Number: 978-1-59433-874-8

Library of Congress Number: 2025946332

Copyright © 2025 Evan And Lois Swensen
—First Edition—

All rights reserved, including the right of reproduction in any form, or by any mechanical or electronic means including photocopying or recording, or by any information storage or retrieval system, in whole or in part in any form, and in any case not without the written permission of the author.

Manufactured in the United States of America

AI Statement

Artificial intelligence was used as a tool to assist in organizing, synthesizing, and refining ideas for *The Power of Authors*. All content was conceived, guided, reviewed, and approved by human authors and editors to ensure accuracy, clarity, and moral integrity. AI did not create original concepts or determine the book's message; it served under human direction to support the work's structure and presentation.

Foreword

When opening a writing workshop, I saw group members were afraid, unsure they should be there. I quickly passed around paper. They froze. Then, I asked them to write a word, sentence, or two about what they were feeling.

Here's what I saw: "I cannot write, oh teacher dear, of English teachers I have great fear…" I read it aloud; we laughed, then we all relaxed. Now, we were ready to begin working through the process together.

In *The Power of Authors*, Evan and Lois Swensen relieve you of fear and prove your voice matters. They do this by changing how you think about writing. They know, from years of publishing, your voice matters. Writing for publication is not reserved for literary giants. It's not about fame, fortune, or mastering rules. If you think a get-well email to a friend, a social media post, or a thin volume of recipes honoring a loved one isn't "real" writing, *The Power of Authors* tells you otherwise. Your story has value beyond what you can imagine now. One story by one first-time author can move someone to act, spark an idea, or transport someone to a rewarding summer at fish camp.

Their unique approach to proving this is clear, sensible, and directly useful to me. Unlike anything I've read, this book takes you through the engaging stories of others, some famous and some not. All succeeded in writing and publishing for readers they may never meet; readers who related to their stories. For example, unknown to me and far from a professional writer, Lenora Conkle, Wilderness Guide, took a chance, a first step, and wrote. She realized her power as author when *Hunting the Way it Was in Our Changing Alaska* was published. Her book captured raw, unfiltered experiences no journalist could have written. Today, you can linger around a campfire deep in Snag River country with her fascinating stories, otherwise lost forever. Another example is a story you'll read about in Chapter Six, the mystery around a rural doctor and extraordinary leader, highly skilled in both the operating room and town governance. Years after the doctor's collapse and ultimate suicide, a town resident, willing to deal with the cost of truth, took the first step and wrote the story, with family permission. Publication of *Cures and Chaos* helped a community heal by bringing a mysterious legacy to light.

If you are dreaming, planning, or just beginning to think about writing for publication, *The Power of Authors* will embrace you and hold your attention. It will show you what is possible through stories by writers, known and unknown, from worldwide to local community. All cared; they wrote on different topics for reasons across a wide spectrum from the value of a simple act of kindness, to sharing the impact of a challenging illness or event, to defying silence, to standing for truth. All succeeded in publishing with a variety of presses ranging from local to big houses.

Evan and Lois Swensen want you to write—to see your writing published, to believe your voice matters, to know the quiet strength of everyday writers. This book will guide you in taking your power and using your influence for good. Your book is your gift to family, your community, a group of concerned friends or acquaintances, and beyond. You'll see in *The Power of Authors* it only takes one story to make a difference.

Jane L. Evanson, PhD
Writer, Editor, Speaker, and Trainer

Preface
The Power of Authors

The moment we realized our words had power didn't come from a bestseller or a packed book signing. It came from a five-dollar bill.

We'd written and published more books than we could count by then, but *Five Dollars* was different. It was born from a simple idea: one act of kindness—just one—could change someone's day, maybe even their life. We sent out copies with a letter and a five-dollar bill, asking others to pass the kindness on.

Not long after, we received an email from a woman who'd read the book. She told us she'd used her five dollars to buy lunch for a homeless man she passed every day. She said, "I realized I've been waiting for someone else to fix the world. But your letter reminded me I could start."

This one message hit us harder than any royalty check or review ever had. It reminded us words paired with intent—and delivered without fanfare—can ripple outward in ways we'll never fully see.

In this moment, we knew: our words mattered. Not because they were perfect, but because they moved someone to act.

If you're reading this book, you've probably felt it too—this tug in your spirit telling you your words could matter. Maybe you've dismissed it. Perhaps you've told yourself real writing only happens in bestselling novels or prestigious magazines. Maybe you think your email to a friend, your social media post, or your family story doesn't count as "real" writing.

We're here to tell you otherwise.

We've spent decades assisting people tell their stories—pilots, fishermen, missionaries, grandmothers. We've seen books written to preserve family legacies, to honor lost loved ones, to share hard-won wisdom from lives no one else could have lived. We've watched comment threads carry more truth than some published novels. We've seen five-dollar bills spark movements.

What frustrates us most about how people think about writing today is the way they discount anything lacking fame, a publishing contract, or a spotlight. When someone says only big-house publishing gives writing legitimacy, we think of authors like Lenora Conkle, who wasn't a professional writer but a guide who lived the stories she told. Her book *Hunting the Way It Was in Our Changing Alaska* captures raw, unfiltered experiences no professional journalist could have written. Because she chose to write, readers can now linger around a campfire 50 miles deep in the Snag River country, hearing fascinating stories otherwise lost forever.

Or Ollen Hunt, one of the last Buffalo Soldiers, who wrote about his life with desire, dedication, and discipline. His memoir, *Buffalo Soldier: What My Country Did for Me—What I Did for My Country,* ensures the legacy of the Buffalo Soldiers is preserved for future generations. Ollen didn›t wait for perfect conditions. He wrote. And because he did, his words live on.

Authors we celebrate in this book—from Dickens to Dickinson, from Tolstoy to Morrison—all started the same way you might start today: with something needing to be said and the spine to say it. They wrote to change things. They wrote to wake people up—and to remind someone they weren't alone.

Their examples aren't meant to intimidate you. They're meant to remind you of the power they wield. These same truths—standing up, speaking clearly, offering hope lives in your words too.

When we see someone hesitating to write something meaningful, we tell them: *If you don't write it, no one else will—and what's lost might be more than a story; it might be a piece of our shared memory.*

We wrote *The Power of Authors* because we've spent years with writers who didn't know their words had power. After working with hundreds of authors, we saw something missing—no one was saying clearly what we've learned the hard way: writers shape the world, for better or worse. This book is our way of reminding them what's at stake—and urging them to use their influence for good.

Our biggest fear? This message won't find its way into the hands and hearts of the people who need it. Our biggest hope? At least one person will read this book, and be moved to write, speak the truth, light a fire under a cause needing attention, and start something making the world a little better.

Because here's what we know after decades in this business: You've got a story. What are you waiting for? What you write could reach further than you'll ever know, and the world needs your story.

If you've ever felt a quiet nudge to speak up, share an idea, or put a thought into writing, *The Power of Authors* is your invitation to do it. In the pages ahead, we'll explore why words matter, what's lost when they go unwritten, and how to use your writing—whatever form it takes—with purpose and conviction.

Contents

Foreword 5
Preface: The Power of Authors 7
Introduction: Writers as Builders of a Better World 13
Chapter One: Words Awakening Nations 17
Chapter Two: Authors Who Defied Silence 27
Chapter Three: Fiction Changing Reality 39
Chapter Four: Literature as a Mirror to Humanity 51
Chapter Five: Writers Who Dared to Dream 59
Chapter Six: Writers Who Paid the Price 67
Chapter Seven: The Pen Standing for Truth 77
Chapter Eight: Authors Who Defended the Invisible 91
Chapter Nine: Quiet Strength of Everyday Writers 103
Chapter Ten: Digital Tools, Timeless Truths 113
Chapter Eleven: Enduring Legacy of Writers 127
Chapter Twelve: Writers Who Changed the World for the Better 143
Epilogue: The Journey Continues 157

Index 165

Introduction
Writers as Builders of a Better World

Stop worrying about whether it's good. Stop worrying about how it will end. Stop worrying about how your cousin or coworker might react. Just write the thing.

We've worked with hundreds of writers over the years—some with world-changing stories, some with quiet, beautiful truths. But nothing tests our patience more than a writer who's always *talking* about their book and never writing it.

Here's what we want writers to understand: your words last longer than you do.

Long after the book launch, long after the royalties stop, long after your name is forgotten, your words can still move, still mend, still matter. That's the kind of power writers hold—to shape memory, shift culture, and pass truth from one generation to the next.

Most writers underestimate this. They worry about being good enough, current enough, marketable enough. But none of those concerns are as important as being clear, being honest, and being committed to saying something outliving you.

What's Changed—and What Hasn't

It's tempting to say technology has changed everything about writing and publishing. Yes, typewriters gave way to laptops, publishing houses gave way to platforms, and bookstores gave way to algorithms. But beneath the surface, the most profound shift has been internal: writers have changed.

Today's writers carry both more opportunity and more fear. There's a sense every word must compete, silence equals obscurity, and unless your story goes viral, it might as well not exist. The freedom to publish has grown, yet so has the pressure to please. Many new writers no longer write to explore or elevate—they write to chase relevance, likes, or acceptance.

When publishing was slow and selective, writers labored over sentences, knowing they had one shot to get it right. Today, the speed of self-publishing tempts many to skip the deep work. Reflection is often rushed.

There's a boldness in today's writing not as visible two decades ago. Writers are more willing to lay bare their struggles, identity, and grief. Walls between author and reader have grown thin, and with transparency comes both strength and risk.

We've also noticed a rise in content to mistake shock for authenticity. Where restraint once guided the pen, some now equate rawness with realism. Power in writing has never come from volume—it's come from truth. And truth, when carefully drawn, doesn't need to be graphic to be gripping.

The best authors today understand this. They harness today's freedom without abandoning yesterday's discipline. They speak boldly without shouting. They reveal without exploiting. And in doing so, they elevate rather than merely expose.

Misconception Holding Writers Back

When writers come to us, they arrive with one massive misconception: they think the hard part ends when the manuscript is done. They believe publishing is the finish line. In truth, it's the starting gate.

Books don't sell books; people sell books. A good book doesn't find readers on its own. It's the author who has to step up, introduce it, talk about it, believe in it enough to share it—one reader, one event, one bookstore at a time.

We've seen excellent manuscripts gather dust, and modest ones take flight—because one author sat back, and another showed up.

Introduction : Writers as Builders of a Better World

Why This Book Now

Despite all the noise, the platforms, the algorithms, and the pressure to go viral, what gives us hope about writers today is there are still many who care more about meaning than marketing.

We've watched new authors pour themselves into books they know won't make them rich. We've seen schoolteachers, bush pilots, homemakers, and veterans step forward with stories worth telling. Nancy Becker's *Trapline Chatter*—a simple, honest account of life as a trapper's wife in rural Alaska. It is authentic. And readers from all walks of life connected with Nancy's voice, turning a regional memoir into something universal.

Nancy never wrote to be heard by everyone—but somehow, she was. Her success reminds us, lasting stories aren't always the loud ones. They're the ones ringing true.

Yet within all the digital noise, a quiet yearning remains. Writers still long to connect, to be true, to leave something lasting. What's changed most is not how we write, but why we write.

This is where *The Power of Authors* steps in—not to condemn the tools, but to remind writers of their calling.

Your Place in This Story

You don't need a million readers to make an impact. You just need one. But you'll never reach one if you don't write it down.

A handwritten note left on a colleague's desk brings unexpected encouragement during a difficult week. A thoughtfully composed email repairs a relationship once believed beyond saving. A well-written social media post can shift someone's perspective on a crucial issue. A bedtime story, lovingly told, plants seeds of character destined to grow for decades.

These aren't just communications. They're acts of creation. And the people behind them—whether they realize it or not—are authors with extraordinary power.

Throughout history, when nations stood at critical crossroads or communities faced their deepest challenges, it wasn't always politicians or generals who provided needed guidance—it was writers—people with pens, paper, and purpose who articulated what others felt but couldn't express.

These writers held no magical abilities. They weren't designated by title or birth to speak for others. They recognized a need, felt a burden, and wrote words awakening something dormant in their readers' hearts.

Power they wielded is available to you every time you write—whether writing a novel, composing an email to a friend in crisis, or sharing a thoughtful post connecting with hundreds or thousands.

What You'll Find Here

This book isn't about achieving literary fame or mastering academic technique. It's about something more important: recognizing the moral impact of your words every time you write, and embracing this responsibility with purpose and joy.

Each chapter examines authors who understood writing carries moral responsibility—some famous, others obscure—and shows how their commitments translated into words changing lives, communities, and entire nations. But we don't stop with historical examples.

Through reflections, we invite you to see your writing—whether it's a novel manuscript or a birthday card—as part of this same tradition. Power these authors wielded isn't reserved for literary giants. It belongs to you, too, in every word you write.

This isn't a book meant to be skimmed and shelved. It's here to change how you think about writing—and how you write it.

The Power of Authors shows why your words matter—and how to make them matter even more.

Now, turn the page and discover the extraordinary power you hold every time you write.

Chapter One
Words Awakening Nations

"The pen is mightier than the sword." — Edward Bulwer-Lytton

Your words don't just fill space—they shape it.

Every sentence you write carries weight. Whether it's a text to your daughter, a note left on someone's windshield, or a post you share on social media, your words either build up or tear down. They don't sit neutral. They point somewhere. They set a tone. They leave a mark.

People who write today—whether in books, blogs, or birthday cards—have more reach than any generation before. But with reach comes responsibility. If your words can touch thousands through a post, or even just one person through a letter, you ought to ask yourself—*what are they carrying? Light or heat? Truth or noise? Unity or division?*

I've learned alongside individuals who understood this instinctively. They wrote to heal, help, and remember what others wanted to forget. And in doing so, they awakened something larger than themselves.

When nations stand at crossroads or communities face their deepest challenges, it's not always politicians or generals who provide the guidance people need. Sometimes it's someone with a pen who puts into words what others feel but can't express.

Maybe it's a mother writing to her school board about her child's needs. Maybe it's a neighbor posting something honest about what's happening in town. Maybe it's you, putting thoughts into words someone else desperately needed to hear.

These writers don't possess magical abilities. They're not appointed by anyone to speak for others. They recognize a need, feel a burden, and write words awakening something dormant in people's hearts.

The power they wield is available to you every time you write.

Conscience Stirrer

Charles Dickens

If we were sitting around a fire and the conversation turned to writers who changed things, I'd tell you about Charles Dickens every time.

Dickens wrote to stir the conscience. He saw poverty, injustice, and neglect, not as scenery for a story, but as people who needed a voice. He gave them one. Page after page, he peeled back the curtain on Victorian England and made readers look where they'd rather not. He chose not to scold—he revealed. And once he spoke, readers carried the image with them, unable to let it go.

As a boy, Charles Dickens knew poverty firsthand. At twelve, while his father sat in debtors' prison, young Charles worked in a blacking factory, pasting labels on bottles of shoe polish. This experience could have made him bitter. Instead, it gave him eyes to see lives comfortable society preferred to ignore.

What I respect most is how he made truth go down easy. He wrapped hard things in humor, wit, and heart. He made wealthy families care about poor ones, not through guilt, but through story. Characters like Oliver Twist weren't invented to fill pages—they were drawn from life. They felt real because they were. And once they entered a reader's world, they stayed.

When Oliver, surrounded by starving workhouse boys, approaches the master and asks, "Please, sir, I want some more," Dickens accomplished something powerful. He made his comfortable middle-class readers *feel* the cruel absurdity of a system letting children starve while administrators feasted.

After *Nicholas Nickleby* exposed brutal Yorkshire schools where unwanted children were sent to be forgotten, public outrage grew, and many such institutions declined or closed. His wider body of work helped focus attention on sanitation and prison reform in Parliament.

CHAPTER ONE: WORDS AWAKENING NATIONS

Dickens did more than amuse crowds—he redirected them. His work pushed reforms in child labor, debtors' prisons, and education. Not because he preached, but because he cared. And when someone cares deeply enough, readers notice.

Think about the impact: A man who began by writing stories to entertain saved children from abuse and neglect—not through political power but through words, making people care.

I see this same voice in authors we've published—especially Carl Douglass. Carl writes with a surgeon's precision and a reformer's conscience. His books don't just tell a story—they press readers to examine power, ethics, and truth. In *The Last Phoenix*, Carl doesn't romanticize espionage or heroism. He follows a young man through disillusionment, betrayal, and moral reckoning. It's not fiction for the sake of plot—it's fiction meant to say something deeper.

Carl doesn't follow literary fashion. He writes from conviction. He sees the cost of silence and speaks anyway. When I read Dickens, I see this same urgency. This same refusal to look away.

When you see something wrong—really wrong—you have the same ability Dickens used. You don't need political office to make people care about what they've ignored. Maybe it's a letter to the school board about a child's needs. Maybe it's a post about what's happening in town. Maybe it's an email finally naming what everyone knows but won't say.

The question isn't whether you can make injustice visible—it's whether you'll use this power when the moment calls. Writing with conscience means understanding your responsibility extends beyond yourself. When you write to serve something larger—to help, to heal, to honor—your words carry weight clever technique can't manufacture.

REVOLUTION THROUGH FAMILY STORIES

Louisa May Alcott

Louisa May Alcott grew up on the edge of financial disaster. Her father, a philosopher who prioritized ideals over income, couldn't put food on the table. To support her struggling family, Alcott wrote whatever would sell—gothic thrillers, sensation stories, and finally, at her publisher's request, "a girls' story."

The girls' story became *Little Women* (1868), a novel quietly revolutionizing American womanhood while giving the impression of a simple family tale. Through Jo March, Alcott created a young woman who defied convention—choosing writing over marriage, cutting her hair to support her family, and insisting on her right to be angry, ambitious, and imperfect.

"I want to do something splendid... something heroic or wonderful—something living on after I'm dead," Jo declares. This statement challenged an era when women's highest aspirations were supposed to be marriage and motherhood. Without directly attacking social norms, Alcott expanded what generations of girls believed possible for their lives.

Alcott's strength was in making her revolution palatable. By embedding her challenges to gender norms within a loving family story, she slipped radical ideas past readers' defenses. The book looked safe enough to be welcomed into Victorian households while planting seeds of expanded possibilities for girls.

Revolutionary writing often looks harmless on the surface. Think about it: your bedtime story quietly shows a daughter she can be anything. Your holiday letter celebrates an unconventional family structure. Your graduation card expands what a young person believes is possible. Alcott understood change happens best when it doesn't feel threatening. When you embed big ideas in familiar packages, you slip past people's defenses and plant seeds growing when they're ready. Truth delivered with wisdom and care often reaches hearts arguments cannot touch.

Wisdom for a New Nation

Benjamin Franklin

Benjamin Franklin wasn't born to privilege—he was the fifteenth child of a soap maker who could only afford to send him to school for two years. Yet he became one of the most influential voices in shaping American identity through reading, writing, and publishing.

Franklin understood a revolution might be won on battlefields, but a nation is built through shared values. His *Poor Richard's Almanack*, published annually from 1732 to 1758, taught principles of thrift, industry, and practical virtue through simple sayings crossing class and educational boundaries. "Early to bed and early to rise, makes a man healthy, wealthy, and wise" wasn't just advice—it defined American character.

His famous words, "Those who would give up essential Liberty, to purchase a little temporary Safety, deserve neither Liberty nor Safety," wasn't just political observation but a moral principle still framing American debates on freedom and security centuries later.

Impact came through clarity and accessibility. He delivered profound truths in straightforward language, becoming part of everyday speech. He wasn't writing for the educated elite but for ordinary citizens building a new nation.

Franklin knew something most people miss: nations aren't built by politicians—they're built by shared values, one conversation at a time. Every thank-you note defining what your company stands for. Every neighborhood post reminding people why they chose to live there. Every family story passing principles from one generation to the next. This is how communities form their identity. Not through grand speeches, but through daily work of people who take time to articulate what matters.

LANGUAGE OF WARNING

George Orwell

When George Orwell wrote *1984* and *Animal Farm*, he wasn't just creating entertaining fiction—he was fashioning a vocabulary for recognizing tyranny in its earliest stages. Having witnessed totalitarianism's rise firsthand during the Spanish Civil War, Orwell created stories readers recognized as dangerous patterns of political manipulation.

Through concepts like "doublethink," "Newspeak," and "thoughtcrime," Orwell gave readers tools to identify threats to freedom across eras and political systems. When Winston Smith reflects, "He who controls the past controls the future. He who controls the present controls the past," Orwell provides language enabling us to recognize propaganda's mechanisms.

Orwell understood warning signs of tyranny often hide in plain sight, disguised as progress or security. His skill was precision—naming dangers so clearly readers gained the ability to recognize totalitarian patterns in any context.

He showed how political language can hide wrongdoing—how it can "make lies sound truthful and murder respectable," training readers to watch how words are used to mask power. *1984* still jumps to bestseller lists during political controversies, not because it's entertaining, but because it provides essential tools for recognizing subtle threats to truth and freedom.

I've known people who carry this same unflinching honesty. Frank Prewitt reminded me of Orwell when I first read his book *Last Bridge to Nowhere* about Alaska's political history. Frank had the background—former state commissioner, lawyer, insider—to know exactly what he was talking about. But instead of keeping quiet, he put it in writing.

Frank made no attempt to sensationalize. He saw no need to exaggerate. He laid out facts and let the weight of those facts do the work. And in doing so, he became a witness—naming patterns others sense but cannot articulate.

Orwell's warning isn't just about totalitarian governments—it's about any time language gets twisted to hide the truth. I see this everywhere today: corporate memo saying 'rightsizing' instead of 'firing people,' political speech sounding important but meaning nothing.

Your reflective email lets colleagues recognize unhealthy workplace dynamics. Your letter to the editor may clarify what's at stake in a community decision. Your social media post might cut through confusion and point directly to core principles. When you write with precision—when you call things by their real names—you're doing what Orwell did. You're giving people tools to recognize when someone's trying to fool them.

Moral Vision Beyond Politics

Leo Tolstoy

Count Leo Tolstoy was born to immense privilege in Imperial Russia, yet developed a moral vision challenging every institution of his society—church, state, military, and aristocracy. His journey from wealthy nobleman to radical moral philosopher demonstrates how writing transforms not just readers but also the writer.

While best known for the sweeping epics *War and Peace* and *Anna Karenina*, Tolstoy's moral writings had perhaps even greater impact. His vision of nonviolent resistance and spiritual renewal directly influenced Mahatma Gandhi and later Martin Luther King Jr., shaping peaceful movements transforming nations.

Tolstoy's influence extended beyond literature because he wrote from moral clarity rather than political convenience. He criticized his opponents and his own class, demonstrating honest truth-telling begins with uncomfortable self-examination.

Powerful moral guidance often comes from those who examine themselves as rigorously as they examine society. People listen when they know you're willing to be honest about your own struggles first. A family letter admitting your mistakes before addressing someone else's. A work email acknowledging your role in a problem before proposing solutions. A personal post where you wrestle with something you're still figuring out. When people see you're not just pointing fingers but examining your own heart, your words carry weight, perfectly polished advice never could.

POWER WE'VE WITNESSED

I've seen this awakening power firsthand. Not just in the books we've published, but in our own experience behind the microphone.

During our time with *Alaska Outdoors Radio Magazine*, we featured voices in the thick of Alaska's subsistence rights debate. One episode included Representative Beverly Masek, who brought the issue home in a way few others could. But what made the conversation last wasn't just what she said—it was how Alaskans heard it. They heard someone standing up for a way of life slipping through government fingers.

We called Senator Robin Taylor and Representative Scott Ogan patriots—not because we agreed on every point, but because they stood against federal overreach. They defended state sovereignty and equal access, even when it wasn't politically easy.

Our role wasn't to pass laws. Our role was to hand the mic to voices needing to be heard—and, to say what needed saying when no one else would. When those editorials aired, we heard from listeners who had never considered the bigger picture. They told us, "I see it differently now."

This is the power of writing—even when spoken. It stirs the mind. It pushes conversations forward. And opens the eyes of people who thought they already knew where they stood.

Your Awakening Power

Those in this chapter changed nothing through privilege or rare circumstance. Their power came from moral clarity to speak—qualities within reach for anyone who puts words on a page.

None of these writers held political office. None commanded armies. Yet all of them shaped societies—by calling people to remember what they valued, fear what they could become, and envision what they might yet be.

What these writers shared wasn't literary genius or perfect character. It was purpose and conscience. They believed writing carried moral responsibility. They believed words, when spoken in season, could shift the course of lives and nations.

Today's world is no less fragile, and its divisions are no less deep. But the pen is no less powerful. Writers today don't need to invent new ideologies to be influential. They need only to write with clarity, compassion, and courage.

What frustrates me most isn't bad writing—it's wasted potential. I see people who have the skill, the experience, the audience... and they use it all to chase attention instead of offering something real. They write to stir outrage, not insight. They trade permanence for clicks.

The world doesn't need louder writers. It needs braver ones.

Your responsibility isn't to be seen. It's to see clearly—and to write so others can too.

Most importantly, people who write today must not lose heart when silence follows their words. Dickens had no way of knowing which social reforms his stories would spark. Orwell saw no measure of how his warnings would sharpen political vigilance. Alcott died long before countless women drew strength from Jo March. Tolstoy went to his grave unaware of the peaceful movements his essays ignited. But they wrote anyway. They wrote to speak truth—not to be heard. And the world changed.

There are truths worth defending, values worth lifting, and stories needing to be told.

And there are writers—perhaps unknown, perhaps unrecognized—who will rise to meet the need.

If you're reading this, you might be the writer I'm talking about.

Reflection: Awakening Through Your Words

People you've just heard about wrote not for praise. They wrote to wake others up.

Dickens gave faces to the forgotten. Alcott shifted what girls believed was possible. Orwell warned us when language betrays liberty. Tolstoy searched his soul and invited the world to do the same.

Their words reached past headlines and speeches, into the quiet places where conscience stirs.

What about you?

Where do you see something worth awakening—a neighbor's compassion, a family's forgotten value, a community's moral sleep?

It doesn't take a platform or a publishing deal. It takes noticing. Feeling the weight of something left unsaid—and choosing to say it with clarity and care.

Maybe it's a personal letter naming a hurt no one has dared to mention. A story making unseen lives visible. A reflection guiding someone to understand a quiet truth long resisted.

History remembers the movements. But before the marches, laws, and turning points, there was always a voice—just one—telling the truth with enough warmth, strength, or surprise to awaken something in others.

This voice could be yours.

Chapter Two
Authors Who Defied Silence

"Courage is the most important of all the virtues because without courage, you can't practice any other virtue consistently." — Maya Angelou

In the first chapter, you saw how words can wake entire nations—how the right words at the right time can stir something in people who hadn't realized they were asleep. But what happens when the cost of writing isn't just a bad review or being ignored? What happens when speaking up might cost you everything?

Sometimes the truth needs to be told. But how we tell it matters.

I've stood with those who faced real consequences for speaking up. Government pressure. Family opposition. Professional risk. Legal threats. Each time, we ask the same questions: What's your goal? Is it to expose? To inform? To heal? Because when words are both honest and responsible, they can do real good.

But first, you have to be willing to speak.

When tyranny tightens its grip, those who write are often among the first to feel the pressure. Dictators understand something readers forget: words possess a staying power no weapon can match. A writer's pen records what bullets cannot silence and remembers what prisons cannot contain.

This tells the story of voices who were told to stay silent—and refused. They wrote under totalitarian regimes. They wrote despite persecution. They wrote when the cost was exile, imprisonment, or worse. These aren't cautionary tales; they're reminders the price of silence is often greater than the cost of speaking out.

I've seen this in our own work—writers who chose truth over comfort, who spoke when others stayed quiet, who understood their words carried weight others feared to bear.

Light in the Darkness

C.S. Lewis

When darkness covered Europe during World War II, C.S. Lewis's voice rang out with unusual clarity. Though best known today for his children's books and Christian apologetics, Lewis recognized the battle against totalitarianism wasn't merely military but spiritual and intellectual.

Lewis had witnessed the horrors of trench warfare firsthand during World War I. He understood how ideologies could dehumanize both their victims and adherents. Rather than staying safely in his academic tower at Oxford, he stepped into the public square through radio broadcasts, essays, and fiction, challenging the dehumanizing philosophies of his time.

In his essay *The Poison of Subjectivism*, Lewis defended objective moral truth against relativism: "A dogmatic belief in objective value is necessary to the very idea of a rule which is not tyranny, or obedience which is not slavery." This defense of universal moral principles directly countered ideologies making the state or race the arbiter of morality.

His most subversive work may have been allegorical. In *The Lion, the Witch, and the Wardrobe*, he created a story in which children recognize evil and stand against it even when adults fail to see it. The White Witch's winter without Christmas—where it is "always winter and never Christmas"—captured the spiritual barrenness of totalitarian regimes in a way children could understand.

Imagination can bypass intellectual defenses. Through story, Lewis found he could illuminate truth in ways direct argument could never reach. Images, stories, and imagination often carry what arguments alone cannot.

Sometimes the most dangerous thing you can do is offer hope when everyone else has given up. Lewis knew this. He did more than argue against the darkness of his time—he lit candles. Your encouraging text sent to someone who's struggling. A work email finding a new way to explain an old problem. A family story showing kids how to recognize good and evil. This isn't just communication—it's resistance against despair. When everyone around you is losing heart, your words become a form of warfare.

Here's what I've learned: when you write from deep belief about what's true and right, your words carry authority even when they come wrapped in story or metaphor. Truth has power to persuade, especially when delivered with wisdom and care.

Preserving Humanity in Hiding

Anne Frank

Anne Frank, a Jewish teenager hiding from Nazi persecution in Amsterdam, wrote without knowing if her words would outlive her. They did, becoming one of history's most widely read books and a testament to her resilience under unimaginable pressure.

Frank's diary, written between 1942 and 1944, documents the daily life of eight people hiding in the *Secret Annex*, a concealed section of her father's business premises. What makes her writing extraordinary isn't just its circumstances but its quality—keen observations, emotional honesty, and growing sophistication developed while living in constant fear of discovery.

"I can shake off everything as I write; my sorrows disappear, my courage is reborn," Frank wrote. For Anne, writing wasn't merely documentation but survival—a way to preserve psychological and spiritual integrity while physical freedom was restricted entirely.

Despite the threat of discovery hanging over her daily, Anne believed in people's goodness. "In spite of everything, I still believe people are good at heart," she wrote. Her most profound act of resistance was this assertion of hope in the face of systematic dehumanization.

Anne Frank could have written about politics or war strategy. Instead, she wrote about crushes and arguments with her sister. This made her dangerous—she showed the world Nazis weren't just killing statistics. They were killing girls who dreamed about becoming writers.

Her diary proves something important: when the world tries to turn people into numbers, your words become acts of rebellion. Each time you insist on someone's full humanity—in a job reference going beyond statistics, in a social media post showing the person behind the headline, in a letter refusing to reduce someone to their worst moment—you're saying this person matters, regardless of what others think. When everything around you tries to reduce people to statistics or categories, your words remind the world, each person carries inherent worth.

WRITING THROUGH OPPOSITION

Victor Hugo

Victor Hugo knew the cost of telling the truth and wrote anyway. When Napoleon III seized power in 1851, Hugo could have remained silent and preserved his privileged position. Instead, he published scathing critiques, calling the emperor a traitor to France and democracy. For this defiance, he was forced to flee France, spending nineteen years in exile.

Hugo's example reminds me of T. Martin O'Neil. When we published *Into the Fire*, I knew it wouldn't be a casual read. T. Martin served as an Operational Intelligence Specialist—a field operative who saw and did things most of us couldn't imagine. Because of where he'd been and what he knew, the government preferred he remain silent. Or at least, not to tell the whole story.

But he felt a responsibility—not to spill secrets, but to speak truth. He carried the weight of silence for years. Then he chose to speak. Not out of rebellion, but out of loyalty—to the country he served, and to the men and women who deserved to have their stories honored.

Publishing O'Neil's work wasn't easy. It wasn't safe. But it was right. Some writers use words to decorate the page. Others use them to open locked doors. T. Martin O'Neil is one of those. So was Victor Hugo.

Hugo understood writing could serve as a form of resistance when other forms were impossible. In exile, deprived of direct political influence, his words crossed borders Napoleon's censors couldn't control. "… one can resist the invasion of armies; one cannot resist the invasion of ideas," he wrote, declaring the ultimate power of truth over force.

Chapter Two : Authors Who Defied Silence

He understood something about courage: the pen is your only weapon. When speaking up directly would cost you everything, your written words can still cross lines others can't control. I've seen this in people who couldn't speak publicly but could write privately. Letters eventually changing family dynamics. Emails documenting problems for future investigators. Journals preserving truth until it was safe to share. Courage to write what you can't yet say aloud carries the same spirit Hugo showed in exile. You may face circumstances where direct action looks impossible, but your words can still cross barriers others cannot control. These forms of written resistance uphold what's right through periods when speaking feels dangerous.

Unflinching Truth in Hostile Territory
Richard Wright

Born in poverty in the Jim Crow South, Richard Wright experienced firsthand the economic exploitation and racial terror shaping Black American lives in the early 20th century. Rather than softening these harsh realities for white readers' comfort, Wright committed to portraying them with unflinching honesty.

Wright's novel *Native Son* (1940) broke new ground by refusing to create a sympathetic Black protagonist. Bigger Thomas, driven by fear, rage, and the crushing pressures of racial oppression, commits terrible acts. Yet the novel forces readers to confront how American society has created the conditions for this tragedy.

Wright understood, comfortable stories continue comfortable systems. By creating narratives disturbing rather than reassuring, he forced readers to confront realities they preferred to ignore. His commitment to difficult truths reflects a fundamental principle: love requires us to tell people what they need to hear, not what they want to hear.

Wright's story carries urgency even now. He wrote with the full weight of a society pressing down on him, and he didn't flinch. He confronted injustice with truth, and he refused to let silence win. I think of this same spirit when I think of Maggie Holeman.

Maggie's story isn't fiction. It's real, raw, and deeply Alaskan. She came from a difficult home, faced long odds, and still stepped into roles most people said she couldn't hold. She became the first woman to serve in both police and fire at the Anchorage International Airport. She also pushed for separate bathrooms and locker rooms for women. She challenged hair regulations. She became a field training officer. She earned top gun at the Sitka Police Academy.

She did these things in a system not welcoming change. And she wrote about it. *Woman in the Locker Room* doesn't just share events—it shares the shame, struggle, and eventual triumph of a woman who refused to be sidelined.

Maggie reminds me of Wright because she wrote to bear witness. She spoke when others stayed quiet. She lived through what most would have walked away from. And then she told the story.

Taking Back the Narrative
Chinua Achebe

When Chinua Achebe read European novels about Africa as a university student in Nigeria, he recognized something fundamentally dishonest in their portrayal of his homeland and people. Works like Joseph Conrad's *Heart of Darkness* depicted Africans as primitive and voiceless, mere backdrop to European adventures. Achebe decided Africa needed to tell its own stories.

His landmark novel *Things Fall Apart* (1958) presented pre-colonial and colonial Nigeria through African eyes, showing Igbo society's complexity, dignity, and flaws before and during European colonization.

Achebe understood, whoever controls the stories shapes perception. He often cited a proverb: "Until the lions have their own historians, the history of the hunt will always glorify the hunter." By creating literature from an African perspective, he challenged centuries of narrative colonization alongside political colonization.

Maybe you've seen your community misunderstood in the news. Maybe you've watched outsiders tell your family's story wrong. Your family history preserves traditions others misunderstand, your workplace email corrects misconceptions about your department's work, and your social media post offers firsthand perspective on events being mischaracterized—these everyday acts of writing reclaim the right to define yourself rather than being defined by others. When you tell your own story with integrity, you honor not just your experience but the dignity of everyone who shares it.

We've worked with writers who follow Achebe's example of taking back narrative authority from those who would define them without knowing them. When we published *Molly Hootch: I Remember When*, I knew it carried weight. It stirred old tensions. Some questioned the legacy of the case. Others had opinions about how her name was used—especially outside the Native community.

Molly's story is well known in Alaska, but not always fully understood. She grew up in Emmonak, living a true subsistence life on the lower Yukon. When she had to leave her village to attend high school in Anchorage, the trauma of separation—and what it revealed about the state's treatment of Native education—led to the landmark court case known as the Molly Hootch Case.

We stayed with it because her voice deserved to be heard. Facts stood on their own. Molly wrote not to stir resentment, but to tell the truth of her life—and of a moment in history changing Alaska forever. Her book offered more than a legal victory. It preserved a way of life and revealed the deep cost of progress.

Publishing it wasn't just a privilege. It was a responsibility.

WHEN WE DEFIED SILENCE OURSELVES

Lois and I have had to defy silence ourselves. One moment still stands out.

While publishing *Alaska Outdoors Magazine*, we wrote an editorial challenging the Anchorage Convention and Visitors Bureau and the Alaska State Tourism Department. We approached it with indignation. We did it because they were misleading visitors with advertising, creating false expectations.

They showed caribou and moose outside hotel windows. They ran a photo of a woman in a bikini standing on a glacier on Denali. And when visitors arrived and didn't see those things, they turned to locals and asked, "Where's the mountain?" or "How come I haven't seen any eagles?"

It became impossible for Alaskans to answer honestly without apologizing for something they never promised.

We spoke up. And we took heat for it. Calls came in. Letters followed. The state tourism office wasn't happy. Local businesses weren't either. Wally Hickel Jr., who managed the Hickel hotel chain, sent us a letter demanding to know what gave us the right to criticize the ACVB because the magazine wasn't a member.

We wrote him back and reminded him: we're citizens, we live here, we publish here. And we have every right to criticize falsehoods hurting Alaska's image.

The following year, the state's messaging changed. The next campaign offered no promise of wildlife in every alleyway or Denali from every room. It told the truth—what you could see in town, around town, and out of town. And visitors stopped leaving disappointed.

One editorial. One voice. It may not have changed the world, but it changed a message. Sometimes, goodness comes one truthful word at a time.

Courage to Speak Differently

Courage doesn't always look like defiance. Sometimes, it looks like a quiet voice speaking steadily when the world rushes by.

Kati Dahlstrom showed this kind of bravery when she wrote *Turtle in a Racehorse World*. She wasn't trying to stir controversy or make a statement. She was trying to make the world understand what it's like to move, think, and speak at a different pace—and to invite the rest of us to slow down long enough to see the value in it.

The neurosurgeon who saw her early in her life said, "She'll always be a turtle in a racehorse world." Kati could've accepted this as a limitation. Instead, she turned it into a message. Her book isn't about struggle—it's about empathy. It's about living in a world not built for you and choosing to teach the world how to be better.

What gave her the heart to write was a deep desire to serve others—turtles and racehorses alike—see one another more clearly. This kind of heart I've come to respect most. The kind not shouting, but not backing down either.

Here's what I've learned: the most powerful writing often comes from those who understand their purpose extends beyond themselves. Purpose gives writing its backbone.

COST OF STAYING SILENT

I keep a file in my office—full of unpublished manuscripts. Not bad ones. Not unfinished ones. Complete, important, powerful stories. Some are memoirs. Some are exposés. Some are deeply personal accounts of survival, injustice, or quiet heroism. And everyone has one thing in common: they were never brought to market.

These writers weren't lacking in ability. They weren't lacking in insight. What they lacked was follow-through—the willingness to face criticism, carry the burden of their own words, and see the process through. Some backed out because family disagreed. Some feared how their story might be received. Others walked away when the final steps required more resolve than they expected.

And so, their stories sit in a drawer. Truths they lived through stay hidden—the impact they might have made never happened.

I don't fault them. Speaking up—especially in print—takes guts most people don't realize they'll need until it's too late. But it still weighs on me. Those voices mattered. Those pages carried weight. And now, no one will read them.

In this business, I've learned silence doesn't always look like someone refusing to speak. A voice almost making it—a never-published manuscript.

YOUR MOMENT TO SPEAK

People who write today face polarized pressures—social media backlash. Professional consequences. Family pressure. Fear of being misunderstood or attacked. But I often tell them: "If you're not willing to do what it takes to share your words, don't write them down." Because the hard part isn't over when you finish writing, the next hard part begins there.

Words without a voice behind them are just marks on a page. But when someone shows up—when they share, speak, and stand behind what they've written—goodness blooms when words live.

Sometimes I recommend rewriting sensitive material differently. Change the names. Adjust the timeline. Keep the truth, but frame it in a way protecting the writer and the people involved. Not watering it down. Instead, tell the story in a way readers can absorb, and the writer can live with.

I want people to be heard—not hurt. And I want their words to make a difference, not damage.

These writers who followed their example refused to wait until the cost was low. They wrote when silence was safer.

They showed me resolve takes many forms. Sometimes it's Victor Hugo writing from exile. Sometimes it's Anne Frank writing in hiding. Sometimes it's T. Martin O'Neil speaking truth about classified operations. Sometimes it's Maggie Holeman breaking barriers. Sometimes it's Kati Dahlstrom teaching the world to slow down.

Not all survived to see their impact, but their words did, and they still move us.

Now the question returns to you.

You may not live under dictatorship or in hiding. Still, silence takes many forms: the fear of being misunderstood, the weariness of controversy, and the temptation to keep peace by keeping quiet.

Where are you being nudged to speak? Not louder—but clearer. Not angrier—but braver.

The most courageous act might be writing a single line saying what others fear to say.

History may not notice. But someone will. And in the space where truth is spoken with grace, silence begins to lose.

REFLECTION: FINDING COURAGE IN YOUR SILENCE

Where are you in this process to speak?

It might not be an essay. It might be a sentence. A private note. A recorded memory. A truth offered in a hard moment.

Chapter Two : Authors Who Defied Silence

Don't underestimate it. You don't need to reach millions to resist injustice. A courageous act is writing a single line saying what others fear to say.

Your editor might not notice. Your neighbors might not care. But somewhere, someone will read what you wrote and think, "Finally. Someone said it." Putting voice to the voiceless is enough.

Chapter Three
Fiction Changing Reality

"Fiction is the lie through which we tell the truth." — Albert Camus

After seeing how writers risked everything to speak openly against injustice, we now enter the realm of fiction—where truth often hides in stories. Here, writers understood the best way to change minds is first to touch hearts.

Facts tell, stories sell.

People might nod along to a fact, but they'll remember a story. A good story has weight—it sticks. And if it sticks, it has power where the responsibility comes in.

I've worked with writers who wrote novels exploring financial scandals, wrongful imprisonment, cultural preservation, and community division. Not because they wanted to preach, but because they understood fiction can reach the heart in a way facts can't. When done right, it doesn't escape the world—it enters it fully, honestly, and with purpose.

Fiction should do more than fill time. It should feed thought. It should reach into places readers had no idea needed touching.

These writers reshaped their world. They wrapped hard truths in stories readers couldn't ignore, couldn't forget, and couldn't walk away from unchanged.

Revolutions begin not with speeches or manifestos, but with stories. Before courtrooms and congresses considered reform and social movements found momentum, fiction had already planted the seeds of change in hearts.

But here's something I want you to understand: this power isn't reserved for famous novelists. Every time you tell a story—whether it's in a family letter describing what happened at Thanksgiving, a workplace email explaining why a project matters through a personal anecdote, or a social media post sharing someone's struggle in a way making others care—you're using the same power these great writers wielded.

CHILD'S VOICE OF TRUTH

Harper Lee

Of all the writers I could discuss, Harper Lee's approach most aligns with how I think stories should work. She understood fiction can reach the heart in a way facts can't. *To Kill a Mockingbird* described injustice and made readers feel it. She put a child's voice in front of the truth, softened just enough by innocence to slip past defenses.

When Scout Finch watches her father defend Tom Robinson in an Alabama courtroom, readers don't just learn about racial injustice—they experience it through eyes unclouded by adult rationalizations. Lee's genius was recognizing children see moral clarity adults have learned to complicate.

"You never really understand a person until you consider things from his point of view… until you climb into his skin and walk around in it," Atticus tells Scout. Atticus tells Scout. This isn't just advice to a child—it's the fundamental principle of transformative fiction. When readers climb into someone else's skin through story, they can't easily climb back out unchanged.

To Kill a Mockingbird changed how people thought, because it revealed what many preferred to avoid—but couldn't look away from once seen. Lee chose not to shout. She told a story. And the story still speaks.

Good fiction gives people a safe place to wrestle with hard things. It lets them walk in someone else's shoes without a lecture. I've seen stories—real and fictional—do more to shift perspectives than arguments ever could.

When I guide fiction writers, I tell them: don't tell, show. Don't explain what a character feels—let the reader feel it. Don't deliver a moral—let the story reveal it. If you want to move someone, invite them into the moment. Don't lecture them from the outside.

Chapter Three: Fiction Changing Reality

Lee discovered, as you let people experience injustice through a child's eyes, they can't dismiss it easily. You use this same power all the time. Work presentations using a story instead of statistics to show why change matters. Your family letter helping relatives understand your struggles by walking them through a day in your life. Your neighborhood post letting people experience what it's like to be new in town. When someone steps into another person's shoes, they can't easily step back out unchanged. These everyday stories carry the same power Lee wielded. People feel truth instead of just hearing it.

Humanizing the Foreign

Pearl S. Buck

Born to missionary parents in China, Pearl S. Buck spent most of her first forty years living in Chinese communities, speaking the language fluently and absorbing the culture from within. When she began writing fiction about China for Western audiences, she brought a perspective no purely American or Chinese writer could offer.

Buck's novel *The Good Earth* (1931) portrayed Chinese peasant life with unprecedented sympathy and authenticity. At a time when Chinese people were often depicted through stereotypes in Western literature, Buck's compassionate, nuanced portrayal humanized an entire culture for readers who had never considered Chinese farmers as individuals with universal hopes, struggles, and dreams.

Through Wang Lung, a poor farmer whose connection to his land sustains him through famine, war, and social upheaval, Buck created a protagonist whose experiences resonated across cultural boundaries. Western readers recognized in Wang Lung's love for his land, his complex marriage, and his hopes for his children, and the same experiences shaping their own lives.

Published during significant anti-Asian sentiment in America, *The Good Earth* became an immediate bestseller and won the Pulitzer Prize. It also served as a cultural bridge, giving American readers a sympathetic view of Chinese rural life during a period of shifting U.S.–China relations..

Buck succeeded where political arguments failed because she concentrated on universal experiences rather than exotic differences. By illustrating Wang Lung's struggles and triumphs, she fostered connections across seemingly insurmountable cultural divides.

We've published fiction following Buck's example. *Legacy of the Chief* by Ron Simpson tells the story of Chief Nicolai and the Ahtna people—fictionalized in some places, but grounded in deep cultural truth. Ron's storytelling doesn't just preserve memory. It invites readers into a culture many would never otherwise see. You can't read it and walk away thinking the history of Alaska is only a settler's story.

Buck succeeded where arguments failed because she was mindful of what people have in common rather than what makes them different. Your story about the immigrant family running the corner store changes minds better than statistics about immigration. Your workplace account showing what you have in common with difficult colleagues builds bridges, arguments can't. When you show people their shared hopes and fears, walls start coming down on their own, and readers recognize our shared humanity.

Elevating Ordinary Lives

Willa Cather

When Willa Cather began writing novels about European immigrants and pioneer women on the Nebraska prairie, American literature primarily focused on urban experiences and social elites. Rather than following literary fashion, Cather wrote about the lives she had witnessed growing up in Nebraska—the struggles and triumphs of immigrant families building new lives in harsh landscapes.

In novels such as *O Pioneers!* and *My Ántonia*, Cather gave voice to characters previously invisible in American literature. Her protagonist Alexandra Bergson successfully runs a farm her brothers couldn't manage, while Ántonia Shimerda embodies the resilience and cultural richness of immigrant communities typically stereotyped or ignored.

Cather refused to treat her pioneers as either victims or idealized heroes. She portrayed them as complex individuals contending with difficult

Chapter Three: Fiction Changing Reality

circumstances with varying degrees of success. By portraying female characters who found fulfillment outside traditional domestic roles, Cather quietly challenged gender conventions while celebrating the overlooked heroism of ordinary lives.

These ordinary lives remind me of *Heart of Abigail* by Rich Ritter, which we published. It's fiction built on meticulous research—the story of a Scottish nurse who comes to Alaska during the gold mining boom. Her journey unfolds against the real backdrop of Douglas and Treadwell in the late 1800s. Readers walk through historical streets, hear authentic voices, and come out knowing more than they expected—not just about mining, but about people, and grit.

Cather rejected the idea only grand settings or exceptional characters could create meaningful literature. Her commitment to overlooked lives and places created lasting art outliving literary fashion.

When Cather wrote about immigrant farmers and pioneer women, critics thought she was wasting her talent on nobodies. She proved them wrong—the extraordinary was hiding in ordinary lives all along. Every family story revealing a grandmother's quiet heroism. Every workplace tribute to the custodian who knows everyone's name. Every neighborhood post celebrating the single mom who somehow keeps smiling. These stories matter because they show the heroism hiding in regular people.

Confronting Uncomfortable Realities

William Golding

When William Golding wrote *Lord of the Flies* (1954), he was a schoolteacher with no literary reputation. More than twenty publishers rejected his novel before it found a home. Yet this story of British schoolboys stranded on an island who rapidly descend from civilization into savagery became one of the most influential novels of the twentieth century.

Golding's approach grew from his experiences during World War II, which shattered his belief in European civilization's inevitable progress. As a naval officer who had participated in the D-Day invasion, he had witnessed humanity's capacity for both heroism and atrocity.

When the boys shift from proper British schoolchildren into painted hunters who chant, "Kill the pig! Cut her throat!" Golding forces readers to confront the fragility of social order and the darkness civilization barely contains. His unflinching examination of the capacity for evil resonated powerfully in the post-war, nuclear-threatened world.

Golding understood; truths are those we least want to face. By creating a story ostensibly about children—traditionally a domain of innocence—he made his exploration of human darkness even more unsettling and compelling.

Here's what influenced our decision to publish *Caged Eagles* by Kayla Hunt. Kayla wrote directly about hard truths and wasn't shy about it. The story unfolds in a rehabilitation prison where people are often held without trial, misdiagnosed, or medicated into compliance. It's a fictional setting, but the issues it raises—wrongful imprisonment, systemic abuse, mental health struggles—are very real.

We approached the material with a shared goal: to tell the truth through story. This wasn't just about plot or pacing—it was about letting readers walk through injustice, manipulation, and survival without looking away. Stories such as this remind us why fiction matters. Not because it pretends, but because it reveals.

Golding forced people to confront something they avoided facing and showed how quickly things fall apart. He did it through a story about children, which made it impossible to dismiss. You use this same approach when you need to address difficult truths. A family story finally talking about addiction without sugar-coating it. A workplace account showing how good people can enable bad systems. When you wrap hard truths in real stories, people can handle more reality than they thought they could. These honest stories serve truth even when they disturb comfort.

Warning Through Imagination

Mary Shelley

When Mary Shelley began writing *Frankenstein* at eighteen, she created both a literary masterpiece and a prophetic warning about the relationship between technological advancement and moral responsibility.

Chapter Three: Fiction Changing Reality

Subtitled *The Modern Prometheus*, Shelley's novel explores what happens when scientific advancement outpaces moral wisdom. Victor Frankenstein succeeds in creating life but immediately recoils from his creation in horror. In abandoning the creature he made, Frankenstein commits the novel's true sin—not creating life, but refusing responsibility for what he created.

Published in 1818 as the Industrial Revolution transformed Europe, *Frankenstein* posed questions growing more urgent with each technological advance: Just because we can do something, should we? What responsibilities do creators have toward their creations?

Shelley's prescient examination anticipated moral challenges before they arrived in full force—preparing readers to approach new powers with wisdom rather than being carried along by progress without ethical reflection.

We published a modern example of this kind of preparatory fiction: *Surviving Disasters and Finding Grace* by Darlene Miller. This book explores what rural life might look like if the power went out—went out—for months or even years. Darlene wrote about more than food storage or cast-iron pans. She wrote about what it means to live without modern systems, to rely on neighbors, faith, family, and traditional ways.

She took fiction and made it practical. Characters prepare for disaster, not out of fear, but out of love for their families and desire to be useful when others are in need. People who read this book don't just come away with a good story. They finish it thinking about what they have, what they'd lose, and how they'd live if the lights never came back on.

Fiction explores the implications of trends or technologies in your sphere and changes what people believe about their own lives. Shelley saw what technology might cost us long before anyone else did. You do the same thing when you share stories; people think ahead. Your cautionary tale about a family torn apart by social media. Your workplace account of what happens when efficiency eliminates human connection. Your neighborhood story about what gets lost when local businesses disappear. These everyday warnings might prepare someone for choices they haven't faced yet.

H.G. WELLS

Long before most people imagined space travel, atomic bombs, or genetic engineering, H.G. Wells was exploring their implications through fiction. As both a trained scientist and a visionary writer, Wells occupied a position allowing him to translate scientific possibilities into compelling stories decades before these technologies existed.

In works such as *The Time Machine*, *The War of the Worlds*, and *The Island of Dr. Moreau*, Wells offered more than predictions of technology—he explored their social, ethical, and psychological consequences. When his Time Traveller discovers humanity evolved into two species—the childlike Eloi and the monstrous Morlocks—Wells offers a searing critique of industrial capitalism's class divisions.

Wells understood technology itself is never the whole story—what matters is how it intersects with human nature, social structures, and ethical frameworks. By embedding scientific possibilities within compelling narratives, readers engage with complex questions pure scientific discourse might leave unexplored.

Wells proved something important: you don't need to be a scientist to write meaningfully about science. You need to understand people. Your story about how smartphones change family dinners, your workplace narrative about what happens when efficiency eliminates your connection, your community tale about what's gained and lost when everything goes digital—these people-centered stories matter more than technical accuracy.

FICTION WE'VE PUBLISHED TO CHANGE REALITY

Steve Levi: Truth Through Impossible Crime

One of our powerful examples of fiction addressing real-world issues is *The Matter of Gift Mortgages* by Steve Levi. Steve wrote to expose.

On the surface, it's a detective novel: an "impossible crime" mystery involving a man who dies twice, ghost employees, gold-for-crypto laundering, and a small hydroelectric project gone bad. But underneath the story is a sharp, well-documented critique of what Steve calls one of the most overlooked financial scandals in America—gift mortgages.

Steve opened the book with a foreword, laying out the truth plainly: while the characters are fictional, the scandal is real. Trillions of tax-free dollars have changed hands through gift mortgages—most of it going to the well-connected, while ordinary citizens foot the bill through public subsidies and silence.

We backed it fully. Steve's approach was smart—he used satire, mystery, and bureaucracy gone wrong to draw readers in, then hit them with the truth hiding in plain sight.

This wasn't a rant dressed up as a story. It was a story built to reveal the real rot. And I knew it would be powerful.

COLLABORATIVE TRUTH-TELLING: *QUIET ECHO*

We also published *Quiet Echo*, a collaborative novel taking on the fractures dividing modern communities—political polarization, racism, religious tension, and economic fear. It's told through six fictional lives in a small town, but every page reflects real conflicts.

Rather than shouting solutions, the book listens. It asks readers to step into someone else's shoes and consider the humanity on the other side of the divide. I often point to multiple points of view as one way to achieve this balance between entertainment and meaning. When a novel shows how the same moment looks to different people—all standing in the same place, all feeling something different—it stops being just a scene. It becomes a mirror.

Both *The Matter of Gift Mortgages* and *Quiet Echo* take different approaches—Steve uses satire and impossibility; *Quiet Echo* uses empathy and layered perspectives—but the goal is the same: tell the truth through fiction, and trust the reader to see it.

YOUR RESPONSIBILITY AS A FICTION WRITER

Storytelling isn't just entertainment. It's persuasion. It's legacy. Its influence. And I tell writers to write with care. Your words go further than you'll ever know.

What frustrates me is when writers waste their words. When they use fiction to avoid, rather than confront. We're living in a world filled with real problems—division, fear, loneliness, disconnection—and too many stories pretend none of it exists. Or worse, they chase controversy without understanding its underlying causes.

Every word matters. Not just because I believe it, but because I've seen it. In conversations and in books, I've seen how one sentence, even one word, can disarm a person or drive them further into defensiveness. Such power exists in fiction. But when writers shy away from truth—or worse, use their stories to distract rather than deepen—it's a missed opportunity.

I tell fiction writers, "Don't waste the page. Readers may come for the story, but they stay when the story means something." Not every novel needs a message, but it should have a heartbeat. Something true behind the plot. Something reflecting life, even when the world on the page is imagined.

Give readers a reason to feel, not just a reason to turn the page. Use story to say something worth remembering.

Fiction writers I've worked with understand fiction at its best doesn't escape the world. It enters it fully, honestly, and with purpose. They create stories we know aren't "real" but feel truer than the news.

They remind us every story is a choice. A choice about what to show, what to hide, what to celebrate, what to question: when you make those choices with wisdom and purpose, your fiction doesn't just change reality—it creates a better one.

This applies whether you're writing a novel, writing a bedtime story for your children, sharing a family anecdote to make a point, or creating a narrative social media post to understand an issue. Every time you tell a story, you shape how people see the world. Use this power wisely.

Reflection: Planting Change Through Story

Before policies shift and debates ignite, hearts must first be stirred—stirring begins with a story.

Harper Lee, Pearl Buck, Willa Cather, William Golding, and others—understood fiction doesn't just mirror society; it moves it. A single

Chapter Three: Fiction Changing Reality

character's journey can soften prejudices. A quietly told tale can awaken empathy where arguments fail.

Their stories planted seeds readers had no idea were growing—until perspectives shifted, conversations took a new turn, and, gradually, the world around them began to reflect the deeper truths first introduced by fiction.

What seeds are you planting?

Your story may not march on banners or through headlines. It may be a quiet conversation sparked around a kitchen table. It may be a new way someone sees a neighbor or an old belief someone is brave enough to question.

Fiction reaches where facts cannot. It imagines possibilities facts have not yet built. It risks tenderness in a world guarded by fear.

You don't need a grand platform. You need a willingness to tell the truth through imagination—to risk a story honestly told might create understanding honestly felt.

Change begins invisibly—like a seed buried under soil.

Your words may be the seed.

Plant them with faith.

Chapter Four
Literature as a Mirror to Humanity

"The purpose of literature is to turn blood into ink." — T.S. Eliot

If fiction helps us feel the truth, this chapter brings us face-to-face with ourselves. Here, literature becomes a mirror—showing us the world and reflecting our hopes, failures, and quiet strengths. These writers described humanity and honored it. They held up ordinary lives with reverence, revealing the sacred in the mundane.

Write it straight. Don't cover it up. But write it the way you'd want your story told if you weren't in the room.

Whether the story is fiction or nonfiction, it's never just about getting the facts right or creating believable characters. It's about recognizing every person—real or imagined—is more than the worst thing they've done, and more than the best thing someone else says about them.

I've worked with writers who understood this. They saw the worth in everyday life and trusted readers to see it too. They did not need to raise their voices. They only needed someone to listen.

Writers have always served as mirrors. While politicians make policies and historians record events, writers show us who we are. Not just what we do, but why we do it. Not just the facts, but the feelings behind them.

This is about writers who looked at ordinary people and saw something worth preserving. They wrote about those others might ignore. They told stories others might dismiss. And in doing so, readers see themselves—and the world around them—more clearly.

Your family letter sharing what happened during a difficult time, your workplace email honoring a retiring colleague's quiet contributions, your social media post celebrating the neighbor who checks on elderly residents—these everyday acts of writing do the same thing. They hold up a mirror. They show dignity where others might see only routine.

SEEING OURSELVES CLEARLY
Emily Dickinson: Telling Truth Slant

Emily Dickinson lived most of her life in one house in Massachusetts. She barely published anything during her lifetime. But she wrote nearly 1,800 poems, which changed American literature. She had a way of getting to the heart of things without saying them straight out.

"Tell all the truth but tell it slant—" she wrote. She understood something important: the direct approach doesn't work. People's defenses go up. They stop listening. She found other ways in.

When she wrote about death, she avoided calling it "the end" or "tragedy." She called it a kindly gentleman who stopped his carriage to give her a ride. When she wrote about hope, she offered no sermon on staying positive. She said hope was "the thing with feathers" perched in the soul.

She knew most truths don't always fit into simple statements. People's defenses go up when you approach them directly, so she found other ways in. Your comparison of forgiveness to learning to see with new eyes reaches deeper than any lecture about letting go. Your description of grief as an empty coffee cup somehow staying on the counter captures something direct advice never could. Your workplace message comparing good teamwork to a well-tuned engine. These indirect approaches often reach deeper than direct statements. When people discover truth for themselves, it sticks better than when you hand it to them.

Sometimes the most important things can't be said straight out. They have to be felt. Discovered. Recognized.

Chapter Four: Literature as a Mirror to Humanity

GEORGE ELIOT: COMPLEXITY OF REAL PEOPLE

George Eliot was really Mary Ann Evans, writing under a man's name because this is what women had to do back then. She had a gift for seeing ordinary people and understanding what made them tick. She chose not to write about kings and queens. She wrote about regular people facing everyday problems.

In her novel *Middlemarch*, she wrote about people whose lives were "unhistoric"—meaning they'd never make the history books. But she made them unforgettable. She showed how flawed people could still be good people. How someone could make terrible mistakes and still deserve compassion.

"Character," she wrote, "is not cut in marble—it is not something solid and unalterable. It is something living and changing."

This is how I try to work with memoir writers. People aren't saints or sinners. They're complicated. Sheldon Gebb understood this when he wrote *In the Footsteps of My Father*. He retraced his father's century-old journey through Alaska and the Yukon. He revealed the challenges and mistakes without hiding them. But he refused to cast his father as a villain. He told the truth with respect.

His writing doesn't try to fix the past. It preserves it—honestly, but with the same care you'd want if someone were telling your story.

Eliot understood real people are complicated—they're not saints or sinners, just human beings trying to figure things out. When you write about people in your family letters, your work emails, your posts, remember they're more than their best moment and their worst mistake. Write about them the way you'd want someone to write about you—with enough complexity to be recognizable, enough grace to leave room for growth.

UNDERSTANDING OTHERS

Good writing lets us understand other people and walk in someone else's shoes for a while.

Jane Austen: What Goes on Inside

Jane Austen wrote about women in drawing rooms and at dinner parties. Nothing dramatic. No wars or adventures. Just regular life. But she had a way of showing what people were thinking underneath all the polite conversation.

When Elizabeth Bennet realizes she's been wrong about Mr. Darcy in *Pride and Prejudice*, we don't just see her change her mind. We feel it happening. Austen lets us inside her head. We experience the embarrassment, the recognition, the slow shift from prejudice to understanding.

Austen paid attention to how real people think and act. She wrote about the moral dimensions of everyday decisions of imperfect people.

Valerie Winans did something similar when she wrote *The Extraordinary Life of Edwin B. Winans*. She could have made her husband's great-grandfather into a legend. Instead, she told the story as it happened. Edwin went to California for the Gold Rush, came back, raised a family, and became governor. But what makes the book work isn't the big events. It's the way Valerie shows character through small, steady decisions over a lifetime. She gave readers a man worth remembering.

Austen was a master at showing what people think beneath the surface of polite conversation. You do this same thing in your family stories bringing relatives to life through their quirks and contradictions. Your workplace emails show colleagues as real people, not just job titles. Your posts reveal the person behind the public figure. These everyday character sketches do the same thing Austen mastered. When you capture what makes people tick, others understand everyone has a story worth knowing.

Thomas Hardy: Dignity in Overlooked Lives

While most writers of his time tuned in on city life and wealthy people, Thomas Hardy wrote about farmers and laborers. People others ignored. He gave them the same psychological complexity usually reserved for aristocrats.

Hardy understood something important: every life holds dignity. Every person carries a story worth telling. He avoided romanticizing rural life, and he showed no scorn for it. He paid attention.

Chapter Four: Literature as a Mirror to Humanity

Frederick James Currier did something similar when he wrote *An Alaskan Adventure*. He documented the Alaska gold rush, but not the way Hollywood would. He recorded broken boats, early snow, bad luck—and how people responded. He watched who gave up, who kept going, who showed character under pressure.

Frederick just told it straight. And it lasts because of honesty. Your everyday writing serves the same function. It insists certain lives deserve respect and remembrance.

Seeing the World as It Is

When we understand ourselves and others better, we start to see larger patterns. How individual stories connect. How the world works underneath the surface.

L.M. Montgomery: Light and Shadow Together

Lucy Maud Montgomery knew hard times. She was orphaned young, raised by strict grandparents, and married to a man who struggled with depression. She could have written bitter stories. Instead, she chose to show both the light and the shadow.

In *Anne of Green Gables*, she created an orphan who transforms difficult circumstances through imagination. When Anne renames "Barry's Pond" as "The Lake of Shining Waters," she's not denying reality. She's choosing to see beauty others miss.

Montgomery never minimized suffering. When her characters face grief or rejection, she doesn't sugarcoat it. But she also shows people who find resources to keep going. Who choose hope without ignoring hardship.

Heather Lehe understood this when she wrote *Colony Kids*. The book follows families who left everything behind during the 1935 Matanuska Colony relocation—200 families moving from the Midwest to Alaska. Lehe doesn't dramatize or exaggerate. She stays close to the real experience: harsh weather, unfamiliar land, and everyday trials of starting over.

What makes the book powerful is its simplicity. It lets the facts and feelings come through in daily routines and small challenges. For many readers, especially Alaskans, this book became more than historical fiction. It became a mirror reflecting the spirit of resilience shaping the Valley.

In your everyday internet and business communications, you can write about difficult times without being consumed by them. This approach honors both the struggle and the strength.

What I See Today

Working with writers over the decades, I've noticed some changes in how people approach their stories. On one hand, there's more openness than ever. Writers are willing to talk about trauma, loss, identity, faith, doubt—subjects off-limits or softened in earlier generations. This honesty is valuable. It makes space for others to be honest, too.

But I also see more guardedness. Many writers are careful to the point of holding back. There's fear of being misunderstood or judged for saying what they think.

Compared to manuscripts from decades ago, there's a shift. Writers used to let the story stand. They told it straight with no apology and let readers draw their own conclusions. Today, there's more commentary, more explaining.

When writing tries too hard to manage perception, it can lose the truth making a story matter. Best manuscripts still carry this truth. They don't try to fix the world. They show it clearly, one life at a time.

I've also helped shape books serving as mirrors to specific communities. Dr. Matthew Johnson's *Positive Parenting with a Plan* was born here in Alaska after seeing what parents were up against—broken communication, inconsistent discipline, and lack of structure. The book has reached families around the world. What makes it work isn't just the content. It's the effect. Families who read it start to see their own patterns more clearly. They see what's working and what's not. And they get a path forward.

The Writer's Job

Those who dared to speak through story did not claim to have all the answers. But they refused to let the world look away. They made the invisible

visible. They named what others ignored. They invited readers to care—not by lecturing, but by telling the truth in ways reaching the heart.

If literature holds up a mirror, the writer's job isn't just to polish it. It's to hold it steady, even when the reflection is uncomfortable. Your story might be someone's first clear look into a life they've never lived.

I tell writers: treat every person on the page—real or fictional—as someone worth understanding. Not excusing bad behavior or avoiding conflict, but writing with enough integrity to let the story speak for itself. Write with enough humility to let readers form their own conclusions.

You don't need to be perfect. You need to be honest.

Reflection: Seeing the Sacred in the Ordinary

These writers, Austen, Dickinson, Hardy, Montgomery, and others, held up mirrors not to flatter or condemn, but to reveal. Showing dignity isn't reserved for the powerful—extraordinary often hides within the ordinary. Important truths whisper through daily life, not shout from grand stages.

Their gift was attention to the overlooked, the quiet, the interior.

What do you see while others pass by?

Is there beauty in your family's worn traditions? Strength in a neighbor's unspoken sacrifice? Grit in a friend's daily perseverance, no one celebrates?

You don't need to invent drama. You need to notice the meaning already there—and reflect it carefully, faithfully, lovingly.

In a world rushing past, attention itself is a powerful act.

When you honor lives and struggles through your words, you invite others to see worth running deeper than what shows on the surface.

Hold up your mirror. Reflect the sacred where others see only the ordinary.

Chapter Five
Writers Who Dared to Dream

"The artist never entirely knows. We guess. We may be wrong, but we take leap after leap in the dark." — Agnes de Mille

After walking with writers who shaped the world, we turn to something different—writers who went beyond documenting what they saw and imagined what could be. These writers looked at limitations and saw possibilities. They looked at empty pages and saw entire worlds. They looked at what everyone else called impossible and said, "Watch me."

Some writers see what is. Others see what could be. Ones who change things are usually the ones who imagine possibilities nobody else can picture. They don't just write about the world as they found it. They write about the world as it might become.

I've worked with writers like this who weren't chasing trends or following formulas. They had vision. They saw something worth creating, even when others couldn't see it yet, even when the path wasn't clear. Even when the odds were against them.

This is about writers who dared to dream—and had the backbone to write those dreams into reality.

Your emails, family letter, and social media post showing others what's achievable when they thought it was impossible—these everyday acts of visionary writing join the same tradition.

Seeing Potential in Limitations

Elizabeth Barrett Browning: Transforming Limitation into Freedom

Elizabeth Barrett Browning's life shows how a writer shapes physical limitations and social constraints into sources of creative power. Stricken at fifteen with an illness causing intense pain and physical restriction, Barrett spent much of her early adulthood confined to her room.

By her late thirties, Barrett had established herself as one of England's most respected poets despite rarely leaving her room. When fellow poet Robert Browning initiated a correspondence evolving from literary discussion to deep personal connection, Barrett faced another form of confinement—her controlling father had forbidden all twelve of his children from marrying.

Their secret courtship and eventual marriage in 1846 required Barrett to choose between family security and personal freedom. Just one week after their wedding, the couple fled to Italy, where her father's rejection was complete—he returned all her letters unopened and refused reconciliation until his death.

This painful separation, however, liberated Barrett Browning's work in unexpected ways. In Italy, despite continuing health challenges, she wrote her most ambitious and politically engaged poetry. *Sonnets from the Portuguese*, written during their courtship, transformed her experience of unexpected love after years of suffering into some of the most beautiful love poetry in the English language.

Whether you face health challenges, family constraints, or social pressure to conform, limitations—when met with boldness rather than bitterness—become the very conditions shaping your voice.

I've known writers who don't lead with what they've lost. They bring you a manuscript, a message, a mission—and only later do you realize what they gave up to deliver it.

Adam Freestone did more than overcome impossible odds. He lived with them every day and still chose to write. Adam has Duchenne muscular dystrophy—a cruel, progressive disease stripping him of nearly all physical ability. He's quadriplegic, ventilator-dependent, and by every account, long past the point when most would have let go of the idea of becoming a writer. But he held on.

He taught himself to write. He published three full-length novels—a fantasy trilogy filled with metaphor, imagination, and an unmistakable reminder of his own life. His main character, Hyroc, is different, misunderstood, hunted. He struggles for acceptance, yet leads with pluck and principle. Anyone who reads Adam's work can feel the weight behind every word—not because he wrote about pain, but because he wrote despite it.

Adam risked everything most writers take for granted: time, energy, independence, even the simple ability to type. Writing, for him, wasn't a distraction. It was a lifeline.

What did he gain? A voice. A readership. And the ability to find meaning from limitation. He gave the world a story readers can carry with them—a story forged in silence, written with strength.

I've worked with many fine writers, but Adam reminds me why I got into this business. Not for the bestseller lists. Not for recognition. But for the chance to turn a private battle into a public light.

Barrett Browning proved limitations don't have to break you—they can teach you. When life hands you constraints, you can choose bitterness or you can choose growth. Your journal entries working through health challenges. Your letters encouraging others facing similar struggles. Your posts showing circumstances don't define possibilities. When you write from the place where you've wrestled with limitations and found strength, your words carry power; easy advice never could.

IMAGINING NEW REALITIES

Laura Ingalls Wilder: Late Bloomer's Gift

When Laura Ingalls Wilder published *Little House in the Big Woods* in 1932, she was 65 years old—an age when many consider their productive years behind them. Her path to writing books had been anything but direct. Frontier hardship had ended her formal education by eighth grade.

Throughout these demanding decades, Wilder kept the habit of writing, initially in private journals and later in agricultural columns for regional publications. Encouraged by her daughter Rose Wilder Lane, already an established writer, Wilder began transforming her childhood memories into fiction in her early sixties.

Between ages 65 and 76, Wilder wrote eight novels chronicling her frontier childhood with detail and emotional honesty. Her *Little House* series succeeded not despite but because of her long life before publication. Decades of reflection had given her perspective on experiences she might have romanticized or oversimplified if written earlier.

You may find your most important writing comes not in youth but after decades of living and reflection. A memoir written in retirement, a family history compiled for grandchildren, a community newsletter capturing disappearing local knowledge often carry special value because they come from accumulated experience and perspective impossible in youth. Wisdom coming from living a long life—whether it's in a graduation card to your niece or a retirement speech to your colleagues—carries weight your younger words never could. You've seen patterns others haven't noticed yet. You've watched trends come and go. When you share what you've learned from decades of paying attention, people listen differently.

Mary Flint: Building Universes from Scratch

If I had to choose one writer in our catalog who embodies "daring to dream," it would be Mary Flint. She was just sixteen when she began building an entire universe—one not borrowed or adapted, but forged from scratch. Stirred by storytelling giants like George Lucas, Christopher Paolini, and Richard Paul Evans, she set out to create her own world. The result was *Red Star*, the first in a sweeping science fiction trilogy breathtaking in its scope.

This wasn't fan fiction. Mary wasn't a mimic. She constructed. She imagined a system of governance, interplanetary politics, alien species, cultural conflicts, technology, and mythologies—and then wrapped it all around a coming-of-age story about identity, purpose, and sacrifice. From her home in South Texas, she built a galaxy.

Sheer audacity of it—at sixteen—is enough to merit admiration. But what makes *Red Star* stand out isn't just its ambition. It's the heart behind

Chapter Five: Writers Who Dared to Dream

it. Mary's characters wrestle with real emotions: betrayal, belonging, and weight of responsibility. Her hero isn't perfect, and the world she created doesn't resolve neatly. She trusted readers to navigate complexity and kept the tone earnest, not cynical—remarkably rare in dystopian or space-faring fiction.

What seemed impossible for a teenager—writing a trilogy, building a universe, and publishing before adulthood—became possible because Mary refused to limit herself. And I set no limit on her, either. I saw the spark. I saw the architecture of an entire imagined realm. And I supported it.

She proved young writers can be world-builders, myth-makers, and visionary creators. In doing so, she showed the future of storytelling often begins in the audacity to say, "They did it. I can too."

BONNYE MATTHEWS: REIMAGINING THE PAST

Some writers don't just imagine the future—they reimagine the past. Bonnye Matthews did precisely this when she spent five years researching the peopling of the Americas and then wrote her *Winds of Change* series, beginning with *Ki'ti's Story, 75,000 BC*.

While others might simplify prehistory for the sake of accessibility, Matthews insisted on writing with respect, precision, and integrity. She believed her readers, whether amateur historians, fiction fans, or curious students, deserved more than folklore and footnotes. They deserved truth woven into story—and she gave it to them.

Her research challenged the traditional land bridge narrative and shaped those findings into compelling, character-driven novels. It would have been easier to repeat the established story. Instead, she wrote what her research revealed—and trusted her readers to keep up.

Her books won awards year after year, not for following trends, but for honoring complexity. Her characters—intelligent, emotional, inventive—aren't just prehistoric stick figures; they're fully human, shaped by environment, culture, and survival. She wrote for the thoughtful reader, the curious learner, the one who might not have a degree but holds a deep hunger for understanding.

Critics noticed. Grace Cavalieri of the Library of Congress called her "America's preeminent writer of prehistoric history." Midwest Book Review praised her ability to turn advanced archaeological insight into novels both "fascinating, informative, and entertaining." This balance—honesty and engagement, depth and accessibility—sets her apart.

She spent years researching what happened before she wrote her version of the story. When you challenge the accepted version of events—whether it's family history not quite adding up or workplace problems which keep getting the same failed solutions—you're choosing difficult truth over easy stories. Your careful research into what Grandpa's generation faced. Your workplace memo questioning why things have always been done this way. These acts of honest investigation serve truth better than comfortable myths.

CREATING POSSIBILITIES FOR OTHERS

Sara Donkersloot: Envisioning Education Through Story

Sometimes the biggest dreams start small. Sara Donkersloot just wanted to write a good children's book. What she created was *Down by the River*—a beautifully written story with gentle rhythm, regional wildlife, and stunning illustrations by Dale Preston.

At first glance, I saw a solid Alaska-themed picture book. Then came the phone call.

Battle of the Books program selected *Down by the River*, and almost overnight, I received an order for more than 3,000 copies. A single inclusion opened the door to hundreds of classrooms and school libraries across the state. Teachers used it, students remembered it, and communities embraced it.

Years later, the same thing happened with *Out on the Tundra*. Different book. Same result. A combination of lyrical language, Alaska-native animals, and Dale's signature artwork proved a winning formula again.

Sara understood something important: children's literature could be both beautiful and educational. It could celebrate Alaska's wildlife while teaching young readers to love reading. She envisioned books working equally well in urban Anchorage classrooms and remote bush schools.

Chapter Five: Writers Who Dared to Dream

The series ended when Dale Preston passed away. His illustrations weren't just visual—they were vital. They captured something unique, and replacing them would've changed the heart of the work. Sara stepped away, and the series paused where it stood.

But the books themselves haven't faded. They're still in classrooms. Still in libraries. Still on shelves across Alaska. They were ahead of their time in one simple way: they were built to last.

I stood by these books even before their inclusion in Battle of the Books. I believed in their purpose, their message, and their quiet power to teach without preaching. That belief paid off—not as a short-term hit, but as a long-term contribution to Alaskan education and culture.

Sometimes legacy isn't loud. It's a book still being read years after its release. It's a child who can name ten Alaskan animals because of one rhyme. It's a classroom sharing a story over winter break, or a school in a bush village finding a piece of home in the pages.

VISION CONTINUES

Pens behind these powerful truths saw possibilities others missed and pursued them. Elizabeth Barrett Browning transformed limitation into liberation. Laura Ingalls Wilder turned frontier memories into timeless literature. Adam Freestone refused to let physical constraints limit his imagination. Mary Flint built entire universes. Sara Donkersloot envisioned education and encouraging Alaska literature.

None of them knew for sure their visions would succeed. But they wrote anyway, trusting worthwhile dreams deserve the effort to make them real.

What made them visionaries wasn't their ability to predict the future, but their willingness to create it. One word at a time. One page at a time. One possibility at a time.

Your letters, emails, and social media posts guiding others to envision positive changes—these everyday acts of visionary writing plant seeds whose growth may reach far beyond your view.

The greatest gift you can give the world isn't just documenting what exists, but imagining what could exist—and then writing it into being.

Reflection: Becoming Part of the Never-Ending Story

Writers you've traveled with here remind us: vision begins with someone willing to see beyond current circumstances.

Each started with nothing but possibility—and to believe their dreams deserved expression.

Where do you see potential others might miss?

Perhaps your family's untold stories could strengthen future generations, workplace's unsolved problems need fresh solutions, or your community's challenges need new approaches. You don't need perfect circumstances to begin. You need only to believe something better is possible—and the willingness to write toward it.

Your words may be the first glimpse someone else gets of what could be.

Dream carefully. Dream courageously. Dream on paper.

The future is waiting for someone to imagine it into existence.

That someone could be you.

Chapter Six
Writers Who Paid the Price

"There is nothing to writing. All you do is sit down at a typewriter and bleed." — Ernest Hemingway

After seeing how writers imagined new possibilities, we turn to a harder truth: meaningful writing costs something. These writers understood their calling would demand sacrifice—and they chose to pay it anyway. They gave up comfort, safety, relationships, and their health to serve their words. They bled for their art, not because they enjoyed suffering, but because they knew some truths can only be written with everything you have.

Stop hiding behind excuses. Stop waiting for the perfect moment. Stop pretending your words will reach people just because you "felt inspired" while writing them.

Truth is, real writing demands risk. It demands showing up when you're tired. Learning tools you don't want to learn. Writing truths costs you something. If you're not willing to get uncomfortable, you're not ready to be read.

I've worked with hundreds who write. Those who succeed aren't the ones who had it easy. They're the ones who took the leap anyway. Who stopped playing it safe and started playing for keeps.

Writers have always understood their job wasn't to chase applause but to plant seeds. To write not just for their moment but for moments they'd never see, and to keep faith with readers who hadn't been born yet.

Physical Price

William Wordsworth: Standing Firm in Revolutionary Times

As a young man, William Wordsworth witnessed the French Revolution firsthand, initially embracing its ideals with youthful enthusiasm. "Bliss was it in the dawn to be alive," he wrote, "But to be young was very heaven!" When the revolution descended into the bloodshed of the Reign of Terror, Wordsworth faced a profound spiritual and political crisis, shaping his development as a poet.

Rather than abandoning his ideals entirely or becoming cynical, Wordsworth redirected his revolutionary spirit centered on how we perceive and relate to the world around us. His poetry sought to awaken readers to the extraordinary within the ordinary, the sacred within the natural world, and the profound within the simple.

Despite political pressures and government surveillance, Wordsworth continued developing his poetic vision. With Samuel Taylor Coleridge, he published *Lyrical Ballads* in 1798, revolutionizing English poetry by writing in "the language of men" about ordinary subjects with extraordinary insight.

Standing against popular opinion costs something. A memo raising ethical concerns when everyone wants to look the other way. A family letter naming painful patterns others prefer to ignore. A neighborhood post questioning something popular but harmful. When you speak up for what's right instead of what's convenient, you're following Wordsworth's example. Remaining true to your vision often requires accepting these costs.

I've watched writers who understand this cost. Mike Harmer came to me legally blind. Not bitter. Not defeated. Just ready. He brought a manuscript, already shaped by the decision most writers never have to make—whether to keep telling stories when the world fades to shadows.

His book, *How To Go Blind and Not Lose Your Mind*, became a guide not just for the newly diagnosed, but for families, caregivers, and people trying to understand what comes next. MaxiAids, a company serving the blind and visually impaired, recognized its value. They put the book into the hands of people who needed more than a tool—they needed a voice saying, "You're not done."

Publishing Mike's book wasn't just printing pages. It was extending a hand. And what he gave back—through his words, through MaxiAids, through every reader who found strength in his story—proved something many forget: even in the darkest circumstances, the dream to help others can burn steady.

The cost of calling isn't measured in dollars or awards, but in whether someone writes the thing they most need to say—and dares to let others read it.

KATHERINE MANSFIELD: CREATING AGAINST TIME

When Katherine Mansfield was diagnosed with tuberculosis in 1917, the New Zealand-born writer transformed her relationship with time and creativity. Rather than surrendering to her illness, Mansfield produced her most significant work during the final years of her short life, creating stories marked by extraordinary psychological insight and formal innovation.

Mansfield developed an urgency and precision in her writing, reflecting her awareness of limited time. In stories such as *Bliss*, *The Garden Party*, and *Miss Brill*, she captured moments of revelation with a clarity and compression few writers have matched.

Despite frequent relocations seeking healthier climates, deteriorating physical strength, and the psychological burden of knowing her condition was terminal, Mansfield retained literary productivity. She wrote to her friend Virginia Woolf, "I want to work in the margin of time, not as if I were working against the clock."

Mansfield wrote her most powerful work while dying of tuberculosis. Physical problems don't have to end your ability to communicate—they may force you to focus on what matters. Health challenges making you choose your words more carefully. Family responsibilities fragmenting your time but deepening your understanding. An awareness life is shorter than you thought. These constraints can sharpen what's worth saying.

Social Price

Mark Twain: Outspoken When It Mattered

Though best known for his humor and satire, Mark Twain risked his considerable literary reputation by taking controversial moral stands throughout his career. When most white Americans still accepted racial segregation as natural, Twain used *Adventures of Huckleberry Finn* to expose the moral bankruptcy of a society proudly proclaiming Christian values while practicing slavery and racism.

Later in life, Twain became increasingly outspoken on political issues, risking his popularity by opposing American imperialism and criticizing the role of missionaries in colonial expansion. His positions alienated many readers and damaged his standing with publishers and the public.

Some of Twain's most critical writings about religion, war, and imperialism were deemed too controversial to publish during his lifetime. He instructed his autobiography remain unpublished until 100 years after his death, knowing his unvarnished opinions would damage his reputation and possibly his family's well-being.

He wrote to keep his integrity. He challenged the assumptions of his time, even when it cost him applause. That kind of courage still matters.

Not all writing should make people comfortable. Some of the most meaningful words are the ones asking hard questions and confronting easy answers. When we speak up, whether in a workplace email, a family letter, or a community newsletter, we're not looking to offend, but to offer clarity where confusion has settled in too long.

Good writing doesn't shout or accuse, but it doesn't hide either. It brings light to what's been left in the dark. Naming a wrong isn't cruelty—it's responsibility. And when done with humility and respect, it can open the door for real understanding.

You may not be thanked right away. It's all right. You're not writing to be liked. You're writing to be honest. And in the long run, truth makes better ground to stand on than silence ever did.

Andy Anderson understood this cost. He wrote because his life was full of stories—real ones. Stories about justice, mistakes, and hard-won respect in a small Alaska town where everyone knew your name and your badge number.

When he sent in *Alaska Bush Cop*, it was clear he had not softened the truth. He laid bare the mistakes made early in his career. He spoke plainly about the challenge of being hired off the street with no formal training. Andy served longer as police chief than anyone else in Alaska's history, yet he made no plea for admiration. He asked readers to understand what the job truly cost.

He knew his stories might ruffle feathers. He knew putting his name on those experiences meant exposing himself to judgment—from former colleagues, from townsfolk, people he sent to prison, maybe even from family. He wrote anyway.

We published *Before the Badge*, *Alaska Bush Cop*, and *Alaska Bush Cop 2*, each one building on the last. But before we could publish books three and four of the series, Andy passed away. He gave everything he had to those first volumes, and they stand now as a legacy—not just to a career in law enforcement, but what it takes to tell the truth when no one's asking you to.

PERSONAL PRICE

Ernest Hemingway: Creating Through Personal Chaos

Behind Ernest Hemingway's carefully cultivated public image of masculine adventure and stoic strength lay a man who transformed his suffering into art at tremendous cost to himself and those around him. His famous "iceberg theory" of writing—showing only the surface while the deeper meaning remains mostly submerged—applied to both his fiction and his life.

Throughout his life, Hemingway's commitment to writing remained his most faithful relationship. He abandoned friends who criticized his work, left marriages when they interfered with his creative process, and restructured his entire life around his writing routine. "There is nothing to writing," he famously quipped. "All you do is sit down at a typewriter and bleed."

This dedication produced revolutionary prose whose stripped-down style transformed American literature. But this achievement came at severe personal cost. His relationships suffered, his physical health deteriorated through excessive drinking, and his mental health grew increasingly fragile.

Meaningful communication demands sacrifice. An evening you spend working on the perfect family letter instead of watching TV. A weekend devoted to researching before you write an important work email. It takes emotional energy to address difficult subjects honestly. The question isn't whether it'll cost you something—it's whether what you're trying to say is worth what you're giving up. The key is discerning which sacrifices serve your purpose and which might ultimately destroy it.

Some writers don't lead with what they've lost. They bring you a manuscript, a message, a mission—and only later do you realize what they gave up to deliver it.

Dolly Hills came to me with *A Mother's Tears for a Missing Son*, and at first, it seemed like a tribute, a way to honor her child's memory. But the more we spoke, the clearer it became: this wasn't a tribute. It was a reckoning. She wasn't writing to heal. She was writing to survive.

Dolly gave up peace of mind, again and again, every time she reopened the wound to write another page. She had questions—endless, heavy questions—and yet she let the world see her grief in print. Publishing her book taught me—writing can be more than brave—it can be brutal. But some writers still say yes.

Fran Smith-Phillips set out to survive the unthinkable and became a published author. *The Search for Dale's Plane* is her story—but it's also the story of five lives lost, one of whom was her son, Dale. When Dale's plane dropped off the radar in Idaho's backcountry in December 2013, what followed was more than a search—it was a movement.

Fran gave up something invisible but sacred: her distance from grief. She lived inside it for months, then chose to share it. Her writing came from a place of stewardship, of preserving not just the pain, but the kindness, faith, and unity showing up in the middle of it.

Neither of these women would call themselves heroes. But watching them lay bare their loss and keep going reminded me what this life costs. Writing in life isn't about sitting at a desk and hoping for inspiration.

Chapter Six: Writers Who Paid the Price

Sometimes it's about showing up to the page with a broken heart and writing anyway.

Cost of Truth

Some books cost the writer more than time or effort. They cost them silence. They cost them peace. But they give back something money can't buy—clarity.

When Joseph Homme submitted *Cures and Chaos*, he wasn't writing fiction. He was capturing the real, complicated legacy of Dr. Vincent Hume—a physician known not just for his skill in the operating room, but for a life unraveling in full view of the town he once served.

His story isn't sanitized. It walks through greatness and collapse. It explores early brilliance and late-stage struggle. The downfall of a public figure is never easy to witness, let alone write. But Joe did it with care.

Before moving forward, we had frank conversations. *Cures and Chaos* would stir memories. Not all of them are kind. It would raise questions in Palmer, a community still shaped by the man's legacy. But Joe had the support of the family—his honesty had earned their trust. Myrtle Hume Nussbaumer, Dr. Hume's widow, said it best: "For good and bad, this book tells it like it happened."

What Joe sacrificed was comfort. What he gained—what the community gained—was perspective. *Cures and Chaos* gave voice to the messy truth of public life, family legacy, and community judgment.

Sometimes the most necessary conversations cost the most. But they often give back more than they take.

Difference Between Talk and Action

There's a difference between someone who talks about sacrifice and someone who makes it. The first tells you what they're *willing* to do—when the timing is right, when the kids are older, when they "figure out" social media. The second does the work.

Some refuse to learn new technology, and it shows. Others believe just writing something earns them the right to be heard—and they're surprised when the world doesn't line up for a response. The worst mistake? Thinking the rules don't apply to them because they're "creative."

I think of those whenever I tell the story about the young man who wanted to become the world's best fox hunter. He apprenticed under a master, learned every trick of the trade. Then, when left on his own, he caught nothing. The master returned and asked if he had done as taught—run the hounds, blown the horn, rode the horse. "No," the young man replied. "I found a better way." But no fox.

Some writers approach their craft this way. They ignore what works, try to reinvent the process, and then blame the results on everyone else.

And then there are writers like Betty Arnett, who wrote *22 and the Mother of 11*. She followed the guidance to the letter—planned her private release party down to the details, invited her community, and embraced the responsibility of sharing her own words. Result? A packed release, smiling guests, and a successful beginning to her writing journey. Not because of luck—but because of preparation.

Successful writers are rarely the most gifted. They're the ones who show up, take notes, and follow through. Those who reach people aren't chasing shortcuts—they're shaking hands, mailing invitations, reading the room, and learning from those who've done it before.

Stop asking whether people will respond to your words. Start asking what you're willing to do to earn their trust, their time, and their attention. Talk is cheap. Results aren't.

Whether you're writing a book or family letters, maintaining a community newsletter, or building an audience through social media, the same principle applies. Show up. Do the work. Follow through.

Why They Paid the Price

Those featured risked everything—freedom, family, reputation, comfort, and health. They wrote not because it was easy but because it was necessary. Their words mattered more to them than the prices they paid.

This isn't romantic sacrifice but practical dedication. These writers understood words can change hearts, minds, and worlds—but only if we're willing to pay what they cost.

Perhaps you've counted similar costs in your own writing life:
Relationships strained when you spoke uncomfortable truths
Career opportunities limited by your commitment to integrity
Emotional toll of wrestling with difficult material
Financial insecurity of choosing purpose over profit
Energy spent creating while managing limitations or illness

If so, you're in good company. Those whose words made lasting differences accepted these costs as part of their calling.

The question isn't whether writing with moral purpose will cost you something. It will. The question is whether you're willing to pay the price.

The world doesn't owe you a reading. You have to earn it.

Reflection: Counting the Cost

Men and women whose stories shaped this section understood something most people miss: worthwhile things cost something.

They paid with time, comfort, relationships, health, and peace of mind. They paid because they believed their words mattered more than their personal ease.

What price are you willing to pay for your words to matter?

Perhaps it's the late nights working when others sleep. Perhaps it's the strained relationships when you speak difficult truths. Perhaps it's the comfort of staying mute when speaking up is needed.

Every meaningful act of writing asks something of its author. Not because writing is meant to be suffering, but because truth-telling has always required the stand costing something.

Writers who change things aren't those who find the easy path. They're those who choose the necessary one.

What will you sacrifice for your words to live?

Chapter Seven
The Pen Standing for Truth

"The greatest glory in living lies not in never falling, but in rising every time we fall." — Nelson Mandela

After witnessing how writers bore the cost of truth, this portion invites us into the sacred space of persistence. These writers wrote to document and endure—to take whatever obstacles stood in their way and turn them into stepping stones. They understood something essential: the pen doesn't just record truth; it defends it, one word at a time.

Not every decision comes down to sales or grammar. Sometimes it comes down to conscience.

Writing doesn't always begin with certainty. Sometimes it begins with a quiet nudge, a reluctant yes, or a gamble you're not sure will pay off. I've learned something in my decades of publishing: the authors who last aren't necessarily the most talented. They're the ones who refuse to quit when quitting would be easier.

Every writer faces rejection, confronts obstacles, knows the gap between vision and execution, and between what they hoped to create and what appears on the page.

What separates those who persist from those who quit isn't talent, education, or opportunity. A crucial difference is understanding something deeper: some truths are worth defending, regardless of the cost.

This collection of voices examines what happens when writers refuse to let truth die on their watch—when they understand their words carry weight others cannot bear, when they know silence would be worse than struggle.

Your family letter you keep rewriting until it says what needs saying, your workplace email you send despite knowing it might ruffle feathers, your newsletter you maintain even when readership dwindles—these everyday acts of persistent writing defend truth just as powerfully as any published manifesto.

Exposing Hidden Costs

Edith Wharton: Society's Hidden Costs

Born into wealth and privilege in old New York society, Edith Wharton could have easily written comfortable stories celebrating her social class. Instead, she turned a clear, steady eye on the world shaping her—laying bare its quiet cruelties, its polished hypocrisies, and the cost people paid to keep up appearances.

In novels such as *The House of Mirth* and *The Age of Innocence*, Wharton created characters trapped within social systems they both depend on and suffer under. Lily Bart's desperate attempts to secure financial stability through marriage reveal how even beautiful, intelligent women became commodities in a society offering them few paths to independence.

Wharton's ability to reveal social critique through precise detail rather than explicit commentary made her work both elegant and devastating. Her intimate knowledge of upper-class New York society allowed her to critique it with precise accuracy no outside observer could achieve.

She had the credibility to criticize her social class because she knew it from the inside. The most effective criticism comes from people who understand the system they're questioning. Your workplace email exposing toxic patterns carries weight because you're there every day. Your community post questioning local power structures matters because you live with the consequences. Your family letter addressing dysfunction hits home because you love the people you're challenging.

CHAPTER SEVEN: THE PEN STANDING FOR TRUTH

FACING REJECTION

J.K. Rowling: Persistence Against the Odds

Before she became one of the world's bestselling writers, J.K. Rowling was a single mother on public assistance, writing in Edinburgh cafés while her infant daughter slept beside her. Her manuscript, revolutionizing children's literature and creating a global phenomenon, faced rejection from twelve publishers before finding a home.

Even when Bloomsbury finally accepted *Harry Potter and the Philosopher's Stone* for publication in 1997, their modest expectations were revealed in the initial print run of just 500 copies. Rowling's editor advised her to get a day job since she had little chance of making money from children's books.

Rowling's journey from rejection to unprecedented success wasn't merely luck but the result of unwavering belief in her story. "Rock bottom became the solid foundation on which I rebuilt my life," she later reflected. Themes running through the Harry Potter series—the orphan finding family, the outcast discovering community, the ordinary person revealing extraordinary gifts—mirror Rowling's own experience of a change in direction through perseverance.

You may face multiple rejections before your words find their audience: a manuscript returned by publishers, an essay rejected by editors, a blog post generating little response—these disappointments need not define your writing journey. They are moments in it, not conclusions to it.

I remember when Ruthann Crosby brought me *Miracle in the Glass*. There were no illustrations. No artist attached. No immediate pull saying, "This one's going to be a winner." Truth be told, it wasn't a book.

But Ruthann had something better than a strong pitch—she had belief. She believed in the story's message. She believed it needed to be in the world. And more importantly, she believed she could make something of it. This kind of belief is hard to ignore.

We gave her the name of Richard Cook, a trusted illustrator. Somehow—through kindness, persistence, or divine timing—she persuaded him to take on the project. The result was a quiet, beautiful book speaking to a community.

Did it sell broadly? No. We lost money on it. But Ruthann? She found her audience—especially within the Jewish community—and sold hundreds of copies through direct connection and personal effort. *Miracle in the Glass* never became a bestseller for us. But it became a success for Ruthann. It fulfilled its purpose.

Sometimes the story doesn't have to move the masses. It just has to move someone. In this case, it moved the right people—and more than most words can claim.

Rowling faced twelve rejections before anyone would publish Harry Potter. Your letter to the editor might get turned down three times before the fourth paper prints it. Your family member might ignore your attempts to communicate until something finally breaks through. Your workplace suggestions might get dismissed repeatedly before someone finally listens. Rejection comes before recognition more often than we'd like to admit. Persistence isn't just for book authors. It's for anyone whose words matter enough to keep trying.

Beatrix Potter: Creating Your Path

When Beatrix Potter submitted her manuscript for *The Tale of Peter Rabbit* to publishers in 1901, she faced consistent rejection. Rather than abandoning her vision, Potter self-published 250 copies of her book with her own money. This act of creative determination led to one of the most successful children's book series in publishing history.

Potter's journey to writing books had been anything but conventional. Born to wealthy but emotionally distant parents in Victorian England, she received almost no formal education. Isolated from other children and restricted by gender expectations, Potter turned to nature study, developing extraordinary observational skills through drawing and painting animals and plants.

When a commercial publisher finally recognized the appeal of Potter's work after seeing her self-published version, they insisted on reformatting it to conventional standards. Potter pushed back, insisting on the size perfect for children's hands and the integrated text and images she had carefully designed.

Chapter Seven: The Pen Standing for Truth

Every publisher has one writer—the one who refuses to go quietly, the one who won't stop believing in their words long after most would've walked away. For me, this writer was Denny Bache-Wiig.

Her manuscript, *Nothing Ventured*, came to me during a lull—one of those rare stretches when my desk wasn't stacked to the ceiling. I read it, smiled, and thought, "Why not?" It was a good story. Not one likely to fly off the shelves, but it had charm. Denny had something else: pure, undiluted persistence.

She wasn't a literary celebrity. She wasn't chasing awards. She just wanted the story of her family's South Pacific voyage—made against all odds after her husband's sudden death—told, printed, and out in the world. The adventure included shipwrecks, medical emergencies, and moments most people wouldn't believe. And Denny wrote it like a woman who had nothing left to prove—only something left to share.

Sales were modest, but she worked for every one of them. Until one day, she vanished. Letters came back marked "Return to Sender." Emails bounced. I thought the story was over.

Years later, her son contacted me. Denny was now in assisted living, still sharp, and wanted to update her book. Most people wouldn't bother. Denny did. We revised the manuscript, republished it, and then—like a passing squall—she was gone again.

Looking back, if I had a chance to start over, I probably wouldn't have published it. And I certainly wouldn't have reissued it. But I'm glad I did. Because what Denny taught me wasn't about book sales. It was about resolve.

Some writers push because they want success. Others push because the story won't let them rest. Denny was the latter. She lived her book. She chased it to the finish line. And then, quietly, she disappeared—leaving behind a record of a life fully lived, a journey fully taken, and publishers who now understand what persistence looks like.

Sometimes the answer isn't finding the right door—it's building your own. Your family newsletter you start when no one else will document your community's changes. Your neighborhood blog you create when local media ignores your concerns. Your workplace initiative you launch when management won't address obvious problems. When conventional channels are closed, you open your own.

Overcoming Personal Obstacles

Herman Melville: Writing Through Failure

When Herman Melville published *Moby-Dick* in 1851, the novel, now recognized as one of American literature's greatest achievements, was met with confusion, dismissal, and commercial failure. Unlike his earlier adventure novels, which had brought him modest success, this ambitious exploration of obsession, faith, and humanity's relationship with nature baffled contemporary critics and readers alike.

Moby-Dick's poor reception began a downward spiral in Melville's literary career. His subsequent work fared even worse commercially, and within a decade, the once-promising writer was working as a customs inspector in New York Harbor, a position he would hold for 19 years.

Yet even in these discouraging circumstances, Melville continued writing. During evenings after long days at the customs house, he produced some of his most profound poetry, including the Civil War collection *Battle-Pieces* and the epic poem *Clarel*. Though these works found few readers during his lifetime, they reveal a mind continuing to wrestle with life's deepest questions despite literary failure.

In his final years, Melville wrote the novella *Billy Budd*, completing it shortly before his death. This story wouldn't be published until 1924, when scholars began the reevaluation of Melville's work, establishing him as a literary giant.

You may create your most important work without immediate recognition or reward. Your manuscript finding no publisher, your blog attracting few readers, your newsletter generating little response—these failures need not define your writing identity or purpose. Value of words isn't determined solely by their contemporary reception but by their truth, which may require decades or even centuries to be fully recognized.

Your family history might sit in a drawer for years before a grandchild discovers it and realizes its value. Your workplace documentation of ethical concerns might prove prophetic years later. Your community observations might become essential reading during a future crisis. Value isn't always measured by immediate response—important truths have to wait for their moment.

Chapter Seven: The Pen Standing for Truth

Finding Your Path

Henry David Thoreau: Power of Individual Vision

When Henry David Thoreau retreated to Walden Pond in 1845, he wasn't fleeing society but seeking perspective from which to see it more clearly. His experiment in simplified living—building a cabin, growing his food, and reducing his needs to the essentials—wasn't mere personal preference but philosophical inquiry into how modern life was shaping consciousness.

His book from this experiment, *Walden* (1854), initially sold poorly. Its critique of materialistic values and celebration of individual conscience contradicted America's growing commercial culture. When Thoreau died in 1862, most of the first printing remained unsold in his publisher's warehouse.

Thoreau's essay *Civil Disobedience*, arising from his brief imprisonment for refusing to pay taxes supporting the Mexican-American War and slavery, articulated principles of nonviolent resistance later embraced by Mahatma Gandhi and Martin Luther King Jr.

These contributions took shape because of Thoreau's outsider status. By creating physical and mental space apart from his society's dominant values, he could see patterns and problems invisible to those fully immersed in the system.

You may need to create intentional distance from prevailing assumptions to develop your authentic voice. Your retreat from social media's constant noise, the sabbatical from professional demands, the regular time in nature or meditation—these practices aren't indulgences but necessities for the writer seeking clarity in a culture of confusion.

Your authentic voice often emerges not from the center of conversations, but from their thoughtful edges. Journal entries you write during a digital detox. Letters you compose during breaks from social media. Family stories you record during quiet evenings instead of screen time. When you step back from the chatter, you can finally hear what you think.

Oliver Sacks: Finding Your Contribution

As a young neurologist in the 1960s, Oliver Sacks found himself increasingly frustrated with his field's mechanical approach to brain disorders.

Standard medical literature reduced patients to case studies, focusing on what was wrong with their brains rather than how they experienced their conditions.

When Sacks began writing about his patients in a more narrative, humanistic style, he faced significant professional skepticism. His first book about patients with encephalitis lethargica, *Awakenings* (1973), was initially rejected by publishers and then largely ignored when published.

Instead of abandoning this hybrid approach, Sacks refined it. In books such as *The Man Who Mistook His Wife for a Hat* (1985) and *An Anthropologist on Mars* (1995), he created a new genre combining medical observation, philosophical reflection, and compassionate storytelling.

By the end of his career, the approach once considered professionally questionable had transformed both medical practice and public understanding of neurological conditions. Sacks's work established narrative medicine as a legitimate field and awakened a more humanistic approach to conditions like autism, Tourette's syndrome, and various forms of perception differences.

You may find your most valuable contribution lies precisely where your interests and background don't neatly fit existing categories. Professional knowledge you combine with personal passion, the academic expertise you translate into accessible writing, the technical skill you explain through vivid storytelling—these intersections of different domains often create the most fertile ground for original work. Parenting newsletter combining your professional expertise with family experience. Community blog translating technical knowledge into everyday language. Workplace training explains complex procedures through vivid stories. When you blend different parts of your life experience, you often create something nobody else could have written.

Balancing Honesty With Kindness

Agatha Christie

While best known for her ingenious puzzles and surprise endings, Agatha Christie's deeper achievement was creating a literary world where moral

Chapter Seven: The Pen Standing for Truth

disorder is recognized and ultimately set right. Through her beloved detectives Hercule Poirot and Miss Marple, Christie explored the disturbing reality evil often wears a respectable face.

Christie's village of St. Mary Mead, where Miss Marple observes with unblinking clarity, serves as a microcosm of society at large. "Human nature is much the same in a village as anywhere else, only one has opportunities and leisure for seeing it at closer quarters," Miss Marple explains.

What gives Christie's work lasting power beyond mere entertainment is her unflinching examination of evil's ordinariness. Her murderers aren't monsters, but people driven by recognizable impulses: greed, jealousy, fear, pride, taken to their logical extreme.

Christie's novels always conclude with the restoration of moral order—the murderer identified and removed from society, justice served, truth brought into the open. This rhythm satisfied more than curiosity; it reassured readers holding onto hope, even when truth gets buried, it still finds its way to the surface.

Here's what guides how I work with memoir and personal narrative writers. One clear example is *In the Footsteps of My Father* by Sheldon Gebb. Sheldon set out to follow the trail his father walked more than a century earlier—through Alaska and the Yukon during the early years of gold dredge mining. Using his father's journals as a guide, he and his wife retraced those steps.

What Sheldon showed—without fanfare—was how a son can honor a father without turning him into a legend. He showed the challenges and mistakes. But he told them with respect. The writing doesn't try to fix the past or make it more palatable. It preserves it—clearly, humbly, and truthfully.

When writers ask how to balance honesty with kindness, the answer is simple but not easy: Write what happened, but write it with the same care you'd want someone to use if they were telling your story. Sheldon did exactly this. And because of it, his book doesn't just preserve history. It honors a life.

You can use storytelling to explore moral disorder without surrendering to skepticism. Your workplace email identifying problems while affirming deeper company values. Your family story exposing harmful patterns while maintaining hope for healing. Your community post calling out wrongdoing while insisting justice is possible. You can face hard truths without surrendering to despair.

Hardest Conversations

A woman once came into my office with her teenage daughter. She was from Europe and had written a book based on her life—one she hoped would serve as a warning to other women. Years earlier, she'd begun writing to a man on death row in the United States. She fell in love with him, moved across the ocean, and conceived a child with him before he was executed. Her daughter, sitting across from me, was the living result of the decision.

She was determined to publish her story. I read part of the manuscript, and it was coarse. Vulgar. The kind of language pulling readers out of the story before the story can make its point. I told her I had standards. Not because I was trying to sanitize her past, but because I knew reaching an audience required a certain level of respect—for the reader, for the story, and for the truth she said she wanted to share.

Her response was swift. "That's the way everyone talked, and I'm not about to change it."

She left, manuscript in hand. I never heard from her again.

But what stayed with me wasn't the rejection—it was the daughter. She had nothing to do with the mistakes made before her birth. She had everything to gain from a book showing the world something better. Something redemptive. Her mother had a chance to reframe the narrative—not change the facts, but change the tone. She refused.

This particular meeting taught me something: Not every person wants to be guided. Sometimes, the hardest thing a publisher can do is say no—not for financial reasons, but for ethical ones.

There's a difference between someone with grit and someone who's just being stubborn. Grit serves the story. Stubbornness serves the ego.

Standing Against Predators

Over the years, our press has published books by writers from every corner of life. Some came to me with stories nearly ready for the printer. Others had been burned—badly—by companies promising the moon and delivering disappointment.

Since I began tracking it, we've published more than 20 books by writers who were previously scammed by vanity publishers. They'd lost money, time, even the rights to their work. And in almost every case, they believed their dream of being a published writer had ended.

They'd signed with outfits like Author Solutions, Xlibris, Tate Publishing, and others who charged thousands for editing, marketing, and promotion which never happened—or never should have. These writers were often told their books were brilliant before anyone had even opened the manuscript. What followed were overpriced packages, disappointing covers, shoddy editing, and empty promises about bookstore placement and media exposure.

I remember one writer who'd spent more than $10,000 on marketing services and never saw her book on a single shelf. Another came to me after a company collapsed mid-project, taking the files and money with them. Pain in these conversations isn't just financial—it's emotional. These writers feel embarrassed. Some are afraid to try again.

Rise of self-publishing brought freedom to writers. But it also opened the door to predators. I've seen firsthand how these scams operate: fake awards, phony reviews, slick salespeople, and contracts favoring the publisher at every turn.

Our mission now includes equipping writers to spot the red flags early. If someone is promising bestseller status for a fee, if the editing feels like an afterthought, or if the contract locks a writer in for years with no exit—run.

I often tell writers, "If you've been burned before, don't let the dream die there. You're not alone. I'm still here. And I've seen what happens when writers refuse to give up." Your persistence matters beyond any single success or failure.

STANDING FOR TRUTH

If you're looking for someone who stands for truth—page after page, post after post—it's Rick Mystrom. His books came because the message was too important to leave unsaid.

Rick has written four books:
My Wonderful Life with Diabetes
Glucose Control Eating
What Should I Eat?
Your Type 2 Diabetes Lifeline

Together, these books form more than a series—they form a mission. Rick has lived with Type 1 diabetes since 1964. Over the decades, he learned how to control his glucose, manage his health, and live a full life. What he saw, though, was millions of people with Type 2 diabetes were being told to "manage" a condition they could fight. So, he started writing.

He wrote to explain the difference between Type 1 and Type 2. He wrote to show how glucose control eating could reduce medication dependence, lose weight, and, in many cases, reverse Type 2 altogether. He wrote with the same tone he used as mayor of Anchorage—direct, practical, and focused on results.

Rick doesn't make medical promises. He shares what works—what's worked for him, and for many who've applied his principles. He writes for people who want to understand their condition and take charge of their health. And he doesn't stop. He keeps showing up, keeps sharing the message, and keeps putting the truth in print.

Standing for something looks like this. Not a single speech, but a lifetime of steady work. Rick Mystrom writes because the truth is too important to leave to chance.

His four books on diabetes represent a lifetime commitment. Real advocacy looks like this—not one loud statement, but steady work over years.

FIVE PRACTICES OF PERSISTENT WRITERS

Those who stood firm through their writing succeeded because they refused to quit when the path wasn't smooth. Their resilience wasn't magical or innate. It came from specific practices and perspectives we can cultivate in our own writing lives:

1. **Purposeful Persistence** They continued because their words mattered enough to fight for. When J.K. Rowling faced multiple rejections, she

persisted because she believed in Harry's story. When Beatrix Potter's work was dismissed, she found another way to share it.
2. **Meaningful Community** No resilient writer succeeds entirely alone. Thoreau had Emerson's encouragement and land. Rowling had friends who believed in her. Sacks found colleagues who valued his approach.
3. **Flexible Vision** Resilient writers hold firmly to their core purpose while remaining flexible about its expression. When Melville's novels stopped selling, he turned to poetry. When Potter couldn't publish conventionally, she created her own path.
4. **Regular Renewal** Sustainable resilience requires practices restoring creative energy. For some, this meant time in nature. For others, it involved returning to childhood landscapes. For still others, it came through music and swimming.
5. **Transcendent Perspective** Perhaps most importantly, resilient writers know their work serves something beyond immediate success or recognition. Whether through spiritual faith, philosophical conviction, or humanitarian commitment, they connect their writing to purposes greater than personal achievement.

REFLECTION: HOLDING THE LINE WITH YOUR WORDS

In every generation, there are forces eager to blur truth, twist it, silence it.

Writers you encountered here refused to yield. They held the line, not with swords, but with sentences.

Truth, once spoken clearly, often faces distortion, ridicule, or dismissal. But truth, once spoken faithfully, also lasts.

Where are you being called to hold the line?

It may not be a public platform. It may be a private conversation, a heartfelt letter, a clarifying email in a confusing situation.

Small stands matter. Quiet clarity matters.

Temptation will always be to soften, to hedge, to delay.

But somewhere, someone needs your clear words to anchor them—to remind them not everyone has forgotten what is good and true.

Write faithfully. Not because it's easy. But because it's right.

And because the pen stands firm, it becomes a life-saving pen.

Chapter Eight
Authors Who Defended the Invisible

"No man is an island, entire of itself; every man is a piece of the continent, a part of the main." — John Donne

One of the bravest books I've ever published wasn't about politics, war, or adventure. It was about silence—and what it takes to break it. Marissa Conklin came to me with an unpolished manuscript. She came with a truth most people spend their lives trying to forget. Her book, *It Happens Here Too*, doesn't seek applause. It seeks honesty. In pages full of raw memory, she gives voice to what others hide. She writes for the girl sitting in a church pew, silently screaming for someone to notice her pain.

After working with writers like Marissa, I've come to recognize a different kind of courage. Not the kind filling arenas, but the kind filling notebooks late at night when the world is asleep. Not the kind demanding attention, but the kind surviving long enough to tell the story anyway.

Some truths cannot be photographed. Some realities don't fit into charts or headlines. They live in the spaces between cultures, in the voices the world forgets to hear, in the stories nobody thinks to tell.

Writers have always understood their job wasn't to chase fame but to guard memory. To speak for those who couldn't speak for themselves. To make the invisible visible, one word at a time.

Not every story needs a spotlight to be important. Some need only a matchstick's flame. Just enough to be seen.

The ground we're about to cover is about writers who understood their job wasn't to chase applause but to plant seeds. To write not just for their moment but for moments they'd never see. To trust their vision when others misunderstood, and to keep faith with readers who hadn't been born yet.

I've seen writers who aren't looking for bestseller lists but for something deeper: preservation of a way of life, defense of a community, and translation of one world for another.

Cultural Translators

Isaac Bashevis Singer: Keeping a World Alive

When Isaac Bashevis Singer came to America in 1935, he made a choice most immigrant writers wouldn't dare: he kept writing in Yiddish. Not English. Not the language of his new country, but the language of the world he'd left behind—a world already disappearing.

Singer understood something about the writer's responsibility. He wasn't just telling stories. He was keeping an entire culture alive on the page. Shtetls of Eastern Europe, with their synagogues and marketplaces, their rabbis and matchmakers, their deep faith and bitter poverty—all of it was vanishing. He wrote it so we would remember.

His stories weren't museum pieces. They breathed with real life. When Gimpel the Fool chooses to believe people who constantly lie to him, Singer shows us something eternal about goodness. He showed the world he came from with its beauty and its darkness, its wisdom and its flaws.

When Singer won the Nobel Prize in 1978, he wrote about Yiddish: "a language of exile, without a land, without frontiers, not supported by any government, a language which possesses no words for weapons, ammunition, military exercises, war tactics."

Some things are worth saving not because they're powerful, but because they're precious.

I know this feeling. When Ingrid Shaginoff brought me her manuscript, she wasn't chasing recognition. She was preserving a way of life—one shaped by the Alaskan wilderness and rooted in generational knowledge about living off the land.

Chapter Eight: Authors Who Defended the Invisible

Born in the Territory of Alaska before statehood, Ingrid grew up alongside the Athabascan people of the Matanuska Valley. She wasn't Native herself, but she lived inside their world—hunting, gathering, preserving, and surviving by the same rhythms and rules.

Her writing did not claim to speak for an entire culture. It spoke from her own experience, shaped by those who taught her. She offered no romance. She recorded what was real.

Still, when her book was published, it received some criticism. Some Alaska Native readers felt the story should have come from someone within the tribe. And I understand this concern. It's not a small thing to speak about a culture experiencing erasure. But Ingrid spoke as someone who listened, lived the life, and wanted to leave a record of a disappearing world.

Her manuscript told of rivers and snare lines, fox tracks through brush, and the knowledge of elders who never wrote anything down. It chronicled a valley before the New Deal settlers arrived. A valley remembered from the inside looking out—not as myth, but as memory.

Publishing her story wasn't about sales. It was about making room for a voice otherwise unheard—not because it was loud, but because it was steady. And because it came from someone who cans moose meat, harvests wild medicine, and sits beside the river to watch the moose pass through.

I don't pretend one book can satisfy every expectation. But I do believe this one honored the truth it knew. And in my business, honoring truth matters more than hitting targets.

Your family stories preserving how your grandparents lived, posts documenting local customs before they disappear, and workplace emails capturing institutional knowledge before the old-timers retire. If you don't write these things down, who will remember them? Someone has to be the keeper of memory.

NATHANIEL HAWTHORNE: BRIDGING THEN AND NOW

Hawthorne had the gift of making the past feel present. When he wrote about Puritan New England in *The Scarlet Letter*, he wasn't just telling historical stories—he was showing how the past continues shaping who we are today.

When Hester Prynne transforms her badge of shame into a symbol of personal dignity, Hawthorne creates a story about 17th-century religious judgment speaking directly to anyone who's ever felt judged by their community. Specifics are historical, but emotions are timeless.

Hawthorne understood the best way to help readers understand a different time was to show them the hearts beating within it. To center on what stays the same about our nature, even as circumstances change.

This reminds me of one of my most memorable projects—Merle and Elizabeth Martin's *I'm Just Her Father*. It was more than a literary experiment. It was a conversation across time, a merging of outlooks shaped by different Alaskas, different eras, and different kinds of wisdom.

Merle came of age in Anchorage before the 1964 earthquake—a city with dirt-street saloons and the soul of the frontier. Elizabeth grew up with modern pressures, raising children while navigating careers and community theater. One saw Alaska as a land of rugged survival. Others saw it as a complicated, changing home filled with stories too often left between the cracks of old and new.

I'm Just Her Father combined poetry, limericks, stories, and essays. At times irreverent, at times profound, it stretched the very format of memoir and refused to follow conventional lines. And here was the challenge—how to make these vastly different voices speak to a single reader.

Humor became the bridge. So did love. Readers needed to feel the connection between two people who could look at the same shoreline and see different tides—and still agree to write about it together.

Publishing this book taught me stories aren't meant to be clarified. They're meant to be shared. The Martins let each other speak. This kind of collaboration—between generations, worldviews, and writing styles—isn't easy. But when it works, it invites the reader to step into two worlds at once and walk away changed. Bridges between different worlds clarify shared humanity rather than surface differences.

Chapter Eight: Authors Who Defended the Invisible

Universal Through Specific

George MacDonald: Truth Through Wonder

Before C.S. Lewis wrote *Narnia*, George MacDonald was using fairy tales to speak spiritual truth. His stories weren't escapism—they were invitations to see reality more clearly.

MacDonald understood something powerful: the best way to reach someone's heart is through their imagination. When the princess in *The Princess and the Goblin* meets her mysterious grandmother in the attic—visible only to those with faith to see—MacDonald creates a story children love and adults understand on deeper levels.

He knew truth doesn't always travel best through argument. Sometimes it travels through wonder. Sometimes the most profound message comes wrapped in the most unexpected package.

This reminds me of Dianne Barske's *Mostly Music*. When Dianne brought me this manuscript, it was clear this wasn't trendy. It wasn't edgy. It wasn't designed to "go viral." It was a tribute—a deeply researched, tenderly told story about Lorene Cuthbertson Harrison, a woman who shaped Anchorage through music, art, and quiet civic influence.

Lorene was a choir director, a voice coach, a community builder. Her legacy wasn't built on scandal, but on decades of service to others. In the world of commercial publishing, this kind of story often gets dismissed. Too old-fashioned. Too regional. Too quiet.

But I've learned the quietest voices carry the most weight.

Anchorage doesn't have many storytellers like Dianne, and it certainly doesn't have many cultural figures like Lorene left. By choosing to tell Lorene's story, Dianne preserved a piece of Alaskan history—she honored the kind of woman every community needs and too few remember.

Publishing *Mostly Music* was a risk only in the marketing sense. But in the sense of preserving the memory of a woman who led choirs, built bridges, and quietly held a city together—it wasn't a risk at all. It was a responsibility.

Some stories fade because no one fights for them. I'm glad I fought for this one.

A tribute to the retiring teacher whose impact can't be measured in test scores, a social media post celebrating the community volunteer nobody notices, or a family letter honoring the quiet hero who never asked for recognition. These acts of appreciation make visible the invisible contributions.

E.B. White: Writing Up, Not Down

When E.B. White wrote *Charlotte's Web*, he could have written a simple story about farm animals. Instead, he wrote about friendship, mortality, and the power of words to save lives. He understood something crucial: readers aren't looking for baby talk. They're looking for truth told clearly.

White's genius was in treating his audience with complete respect. "Anyone who writes down to children is simply wasting his time," he once said. "You have to write up, not down." When Charlotte tells Wilbur, "After all, what's a life anyway? We're born, we live a little while, we die," she's speaking truth readers can handle—truth they need to hear.

This approach—honoring your audience regardless of background—creates writing lasting across generations and cultures.

I saw this same respect in Anna Jacobson's *Elnguq*. Anna introduced me to a different world—she changed how I understand storytelling itself. *Elnguq* is the first novel written in the Yup'ik language of Southwestern Alaska. This fact alone makes it a cultural landmark. But it's the story—the quiet depth of it—leaving the lasting mark.

Anna is an Alaska Native who grew up in a now-abandoned tribal settlement deep in the wilderness. Her childhood unfolded among rivers, forests, and tundra, in a place so isolated she imagined her small community might be the only people in the world. Her memories rooted themselves into a story preserving a traditional Alaska Native way of life with honesty and grace.

Elnguq—the young girl at the heart of the novel—carries a name meaning both "birch tree" and "strength through flexibility." It also carries another meaning: "one who is." And this is what this story does—it *is*. It doesn't explain, embellish, or dramatize. It reflects. It bears witness.

Through fiction, Anna Jacobson invites readers to understand a way of living shaped by subsistence, language, and generational wisdom. She doesn't simplify it for outsiders. She honors it. She lets it breathe.

Chapter Eight: Authors Who Defended the Invisible

Publishing *Elnguq* reminded me—the greatest power of a book lies in making room for a voice seldom heard and a memory seldom preserved. Sometimes the strongest force is the quiet one.

This wasn't just a manuscript—it was a cultural offering. A way for future generations to hear what would otherwise be lost. And it deepened my understanding of the Yup'ik experience, and the responsibility I carry as a publisher: to protect stories rooted in identity, dignity, and truth.

White's rule was simple: write up, not down. People can handle more truth than you think—if you trust them with it.

LITERARY DIPLOMACY

Wislawa Szymborska: Finding the Profound in the Everyday

Polish poet Wislawa Szymborska lived through Nazi occupation and communist rule. She wrote poems about cats and clouds, about people standing in line and looking in mirrors. And somehow, through these ordinary observations, she captured something eternal about our shared experience.

When her poem *Cat in an Empty Apartment* describes a pet's confusion after its owner's death—"Nothing seems different here, but nothing is the same"—she's talking about grief in a way readers from any culture can understand. Specifics may be Polish, but the truth is universal.

Szymborska's genius was finding the extraordinary in what everyone else takes for granted. You don't need exotic settings or dramatic events to reveal deep truths about life. Sometimes the most powerful insights come from paying attention to the ordinary.

This reminds me of Lilly Goodman's *Candle Sparks*. When a book shows a community what it looks like—not in fantasy, not in nostalgia, but in its full, raw character—it does something rare. *Candle Sparks* did exactly this.

Lilly wrote about the Alaska bush. She lived it, scraped it, hauled water through it, and ran dog teams across its frozen back. Her fictional Candle, Alaska, was rooted in real people, real tensions, and real humor. She gave voice to a lifestyle few outsiders understand, and few insiders ever articulate. The result wasn't just a good story—it was a mirror.

For some in the bush communities, this mirror was welcome. They saw their lives in print—eccentric, rugged, hilarious, stubborn—and they laughed, nodded, and shared the book like a favorite local secret. But for others, the reflection hit too close. Lilly's sharp satire and candid character sketches ruffled feathers. Not everyone liked the way their town—or one resembling it—had been rendered. Some felt exposed. Others felt understood for the first time.

What made *Candle Sparks* important wasn't whether everyone liked it. What mattered was it gave voice to the Alaska bush community on its own terms, with dirt under the nails and wind in the face.

Sometimes the greatest gift a writer can give is to hold up the mirror—not to judge, but to say, "You matter. Your story is worth telling." You don't need exotic locations to discover deep truths—you need to pay attention to what's right in front of you.

Jules Verne: Imagining a Connected World

Long before the internet made the world feel small, Jules Verne was writing stories about global connection. His novels took readers around the world in eighty days, twenty thousand leagues under the sea, and to the center of the earth. More than adventure stories, they were exercises in imagination where distance mattered less and understanding mattered more.

Verne wrote at a time when most people never traveled beyond their birthplace. Through his stories, they could experience different cultures, climates, and ways of life. Captain Nemo wasn't just a mysterious submarine captain—he was Verne's way of showing readers how someone from a colonized nation might see European "civilization."

What made Verne's work lasting wasn't his technology predictions—though many proved accurate. It was his understanding, readers were hungry to see beyond their own horizons. His stories satisfied curiosity about the wider world while building empathy for people living different lives.

This approach—using imagination to build understanding—reminds me of John Nganga Wamatu. If I had to name one writer whose voice deserves a far wider audience, it would be John.

Chapter Eight: Authors Who Defended the Invisible

John's book, *A Blessed Journey*, isn't flashy. It's not chasing headlines. But it tells a story the world needs to hear—quietly, honestly, and with deep respect for where he came from and where he's going.

Born in rural Kenya, John's life has spanned continents and careers. From tending the soil of East Africa to conducting coffee research and plant breeding in Europe and the U.S., his journey has been shaped by curiosity, persistence, and service. Along the way, he built something few others have: a bridge between the scientific and the personal, between African heritage and American experience, between agricultural precision and literary reflection.

But his story isn't just about movement. It's about meaning.

He immigrated to the U.S., not for acclaim but to serve. With his wife, he founded adult care homes—quiet spaces where dignity still mattered. There, among elders with stories of their own, he found new inspiration. And finally, after decades of technical writing, he put pen to paper to tell his own story.

A Blessed Journey is a memoir, yes—but it's also a cultural document. It shows what it means to hold on to identity while adapting to a new country. What it means to see the world through both a microscope and a grandfather's wisdom. What it means to live a life full of work—and still find room to write.

John's voice matters not because it's loud, but because it's layered. He carries traditions, languages, and generations in every sentence. His story isn't just his own—it reaches across borders and cultures, quietly reminding us stories connect us, even when we don't realize we're listening.

If the world misses this book, it misses something essential.

WHAT I'VE LEARNED

Over the decades, I've published writers from every corner of life. Some came to me with stories nearly ready for the printer. Others had manuscripts defending the invisible—preserving cultures, giving voice to communities, building understanding across divides.

These aren't always my bestsellers. But they're often my most important books.

Here's what I've learned:

Important stories often come from unexpected voices. Not the loudest speakers or the most obvious experts, but the quiet observers who've been paying attention while others looked away.

Cultural bridge-building requires both honesty and respect. You can't build real understanding by romanticizing different experiences. But you also can't build it by focusing only on problems and conflicts.

Specific often speaks louder than general. Instead of writing about "immigrant experiences" in abstract terms, tell the story of one family's journey. Instead of discussing "rural life" as a concept, show what it means to wake up at 4 AM and watch the moose pass through.

Some books are more important than profitable. I've lost money on books I'm proud to have published. Sometimes defending the invisible means accepting the market won't reward you for it.

Connection often matters more than perfection. A flawed book telling an important story can have more impact than a perfect book saying nothing new.

Great writers who came before me—Singer, Hawthorne, MacDonald, White, Szymborska, Verne—all understood these same principles. They wrote not for immediate reward but for lasting connection. They defended what others would let vanish. They spoke for those who couldn't speak for themselves.

Their example reminds me: not every story needs a spotlight to be important. Some need only a flicker of flame.

Just enough to be seen.

Your Voice in the Dark

All writers have the potential to defend the invisible. You don't need to be famous or formally trained. You just need to pay attention to the world around you and care enough to awaken others to what you see.

Maybe it's the immigrant family running your local restaurant. Maybe it's the elderly neighbor whose stories come from a different era. Maybe it's your own community, seen through eyes tired of being misunderstood.

Chapter Eight: Authors Who Defended the Invisible

Invisible is everywhere. It's in the lives we walk past without noticing, the stories we assume aren't worth telling, the voices we forget to hear.

Your job as a writer isn't to speak for everyone. It's to speak for someone others might miss. To build one small bridge in a world full of walls. To defend what's invisible until others can see it too.

Family letters, emails, and posts—these everyday acts of writing defend the invisible just as powerfully as any published book.

Reflection: Speaking for What the Eye Cannot See

Some truths cannot be photographed. Some realities don't fit into charts or headlines. They must be named—carefully, courageously—by those willing to defend what is invisible.

This collection of voices—both the masters who came before and the contemporary voices I've published—stood for the unseen: dignity, cultural wisdom, generational memory, quiet heroism.

Where are you being called to speak for what others refuse to see?

Perhaps it's a hidden injustice quietly eroding lives. Perhaps it's an unnoticed beauty sustaining hope. Perhaps it's a disappearing way of life only you remember clearly enough to record.

Your words can give form to what others miss and recognize what has been in front of them all along.

Faith, love, dignity, conscience—these invisible realities build or break our world.

Your voice can make them visible.

Chapter Nine
Quiet Strength of Everyday Writers

"Some books are to be tasted, others to be swallowed, and some few to be chewed and digested." — Francis Bacon

After meeting writers who defended the invisible, we turn to something equally important—writers who build to last. Not the flashy voices chasing trends, but the steady ones creating work with staying power. Writers who understand the difference between making noise and making meaning.

What makes certain works outlive their creators while others fade from memory? Why do some characters feel more real than the people we pass on the street? How does a simple children's book end up teaching generations of readers something profound about life?

I've learned something in my years of publishing: the writers who last aren't necessarily the most talented. They're the ones who refuse to take shortcuts. Who respect their readers enough to tell the truth. Who understand some things are more important than bestseller lists.

This is about those writers—the ones with quiet strength. They don't chase fame. They chase something harder to measure: the kind of impact lasting long after the applause dies down.

I've been fortunate to work with writers like this. And I've seen how their approach mimics the great writers who came before them—masters who understood lasting literature comes not from following formulas, but from following conscience.

Creating Characters Who Live

Henry James: Inner Landscape Revealed

Henry James wrote about what people think, not just what they do. While other writers described actions and dialogue, James went inside his characters' heads. He showed how people make decisions—the doubts, the second-guessing, the way past experiences shape present choices.

James understood; the interesting part of any story happens between someone's ears. When his characters face difficult choices, we don't just see what they decide—we feel the weight of their reasoning.

This kind of psychological realism—characters who feel like real people rather than plot devices—reminds me of what I saw in Marc Cameron's early work. Some characters step off the page and into memory—not because they're flashy or famous, but because they feel lived-in, like men you might've known or hoped to know.

When Marc was writing under his given name, Marc Otte, he gave me *Pray for Justice* and *Hide and Seek*. Skip Garret and Terry McGreggor weren't invented to launch a franchise. They were drawn from real life—etched with the weight of service, faith, and brotherhood. They rode trails feeling familiar to anyone who's ever been alone with their thoughts and a hard decision. They weren't chasing glory. They were doing what had to be done, the way real peace officers do.

But Marc was chasing something—his dream to become a writer. And I believed in him. I published those early novels; I stood beside him, knowing his voice was one worth hearing. Realism in his lawmen, the spiritual backbone in his stories, and his characters weren't just literary devices. They were signs of a writer with something genuine to offer.

These characters weren't built to sell a series. They were built to live on in the minds of readers who know what real strength looks like—quiet, principled, and unshaken by chaos. But more than this, they were stepping stones in a writer's journey. Every time I see Marc's name on a bestseller list or in a Clancy credit line, I don't just see success. I see payment for my belief, for the effort poured into those first pages.

Lessons from both James and Marc are the same: characters endure when they're built from the inside out. When writers take time

Chapter Nine: Quiet Strength of Everyday Writers

to understand not just what their people do, but why they do it. When they respect the complexity of our nature rather than reducing people to simple types.

When you bring relatives to life in family stories through their quirks and contradictions, when you show colleagues as real people in your emails, when you reveal the complex motivations behind people's actions in posts—you're doing what James and Otte did. You're building characters from the inside out, guiding others to understand not just what people do, but why they do it.

Sir Arthur Conan Doyle: Characters Who Transcend Their Stories

Arthur Conan Doyle created Sherlock Holmes and accidentally made him immortal. While countless other detective stories from the same era disappeared, Holmes keeps showing up in new movies, TV shows, and books. What made the difference?

Doyle gave Holmes specific, memorable details: pipe, hat, violin, and famous sayings. These concrete touches made Holmes instantly recognizable, but flexible enough for other writers to

Lesson? Specific details create lasting impressions. Generic descriptions fade from memory.

This understanding—specific details create lasting impressions—shows up in my most memorable books. I often tell writers, "Write so your book doesn't need illustrations; then, make the illustrations so alive your book doesn't need text." *Grandpa's Airplane* is the book achieving this.

Kirk Thomas wrote with the kind of clarity not requiring embellishment. His story unfolded like a quiet conversation—unforced, true, and filled with the reverent awe of a grandfather who still marveled at being seen by the little eyes below as he flew overhead. It was a manuscript shaped by memory, not marketing—a story standing solidly on its own.

And then came the art.

Gita Lloyd and Gasper Vaccaro—masters of their craft, both trained and seasoned in the Disney tradition—took what Kirk had written and painted what he hadn't said aloud. Gita's expressive warmth and Gasper's vivid energy lifted the Otter airplane right off the page. Sky and Grandpa's airplane came alive. Kids waved—they squealed, they pointed, they reached.

Harmony between text and illustration was so complete it felt as if they were drawn from the same pen. But here's what made *Grandpa's Airplane* unforgettable: either element, standing alone, could have told the story. The manuscript could have flown solo—clean, heartfelt, true. Illustrations, even without words, would have carried a child from page to page, from wonder to wonder. Together, they made something rare.

After this book, I read manuscripts differently. I no longer separated text from illustration in my mind. I began asking: If there were no pictures, would the story still land? If there were no words, would the heart still beat? *Grandpa's Airplane* answered yes to both.

Lasting Language

A.A. Milne: Art of Seeming Simplicity

A.A. Milne wrote children's books adults could enjoy too. When Pooh tells Piglet, "You don't spell love, you feel it," Milne packed complex wisdom into simple words. This balance—deep meaning in accessible language—explains why his books still work nearly a century later.

Milne never talked down to children. He respected them enough to tell the truth in language they could handle.

This gift for deceptive simplicity—making the profound look effortless—reminds me of the most deceptively simple book I've ever published: *Every Reason You Should Leave Alaska* by P. Nathan Blackstone. Every single page is blank.

It looks like a book. It's bound like a book. It carries a subtitle—*And Never Come Back*—nudging you with humor. It even includes a dedication, acknowledgments, and a gentle invitation at the end to share your own journey. But once the title page turns, it's white space all the way through.

And here's the brilliance.

Every Reason You Should Leave Alaska doesn't just *say* there's no reason to leave Alaska. It shows it powerfully, page after page. It's a novelty by form, but it delivers something deeper: a punchline so clean, it becomes a statement. A blank volume, without saying a word, testifying to the hold Alaska has on those who know it best.

What makes it work is what's missing. Absence of text becomes the message. Readers are disarmed, then delighted. Laughter comes first, but then—perhaps after the smile fades—comes something more reflective. Because the joke isn't there's nothing to say. It's already been felt.

Only a writer who truly understood the spirit of Alaska could have conceived a book like this. It's minimalism with meaning. Simplicity with weight. And like the land it quietly honors, it doesn't shout. It just endures.

Like Milne's seemingly simple stories carrying deeper truths, Nathan's blank book proves the most powerful statements come through what you choose not to say.

Powerful statements often come through careful simplicity, not clever complexity. When people understand difficult concepts through clear language, you're giving them a gift they can use.

NARRATIVES OUTLASTING THEIR CREATORS

Roald Dahl: Stories Rejecting False Comfort

Roald Dahl never lied to children about how hard life can be. His young protagonists face genuinely scary adults with real power to harm them. But they also find ways to win through courage and cleverness.

Dahl understood children can handle difficult truths when they're told honestly. He needed to create a fair world—where good choices eventually lead to a better place.

This approach—telling hard truths without crushing hope—connects to one of the most meaningful books I've published: *Martha and Eva* by Martha Maiwald and Eva Baker. Few writers have told harder truths with more grace. Their book is a rare and powerful blend of firsthand testimony and generational reflection—a mother and daughter sharing the brutal realities of being German refugees during and after World War II.

Martha's story, written in old German script before her death in 1990, documents a once-beautiful life in Schlesien—a home taken by war, politics, and history. She writes of food shortages, Nazi coercion, forced labor, bombings, and the heartbreak of expulsion. Her memories are detailed and unsparing, and yet they are never bitter. There is sorrow in her words, but never cynicism.

Eva, only ten when the war ended, added her own memories—memories of being quiet when her father raged, of finding joy in dollhouses and picnics, of loss and displacement, and finally, of healing. She recalls horror, but also sunshine. Hardship, but also swing sets and plum cake. Her chapters don't erase the dark; they light candles in it.

Together, Martha and Eva refused to sugarcoat what happened. They kept their pain honest, without reshaping it into something easier to carry. But they also refused to let it become the whole story. There is pride in these pages—pride in surviving, in remembering, in passing on the truth to the next generation.

What makes *Martha and Eva* so important is it tells the story of ordinary people caught in extraordinary events—and does so without drowning the reader in despair. It acknowledges injustice without hatred. It recognizes loss without surrendering hope. And in doing so, it leaves us with something rare: a reminder even in the darkest times, love, memory, and dignity endure.

They told the truth—and left the world worth fighting for. Like Dahl's stories for children, this book for adults proves authentic literature doesn't need to choose between honesty and hope. Strongest stories offer both.

You don't have to choose between honesty and hope. Strongest words offer both reality and hope—they don't pretend everything is fine, but they don't give up on the possibility things can get better

QUIET STRENGTH
Teachers Who Transform

Not every influential writer seeks the spotlight. Sometimes the most lasting impact comes from the quietest corners, where patient teachers create tools guiding others to discover their voice.

Quietly influential writers in my catalog are LaVon Bridges and Alice Wright—two educators who never sought fame, but whose work continues to shape young minds in classrooms across Alaska and beyond.

Chapter Nine: Quiet Strength of Everyday Writers

Together, they created *Alaska Animals, We Love You!* and its sequel—books appearing, on the surface, to be collections of cheerful animal poems and chants paired with delightful illustrations and companion CDs. But behind the color and charm lies a method as powerful as it is gentle. These books were born from their years teaching bilingual students at North Star School in Anchorage, children for whom English was new, unfamiliar, and intimidating.

I often explain to writers of children's language books—success depends on three foundational elements: rhyme, rhythm, and repetition. LaVon and Alice understood this intuitively. Every chant they wrote carried a cadence children could feel. Rhyme gave them cues. Rhythm made the words stick. Repetition gave them mastery. What began as oral language practice evolved into reading, and reading became confidence.

Their poems were designed to be bridges—ways for children from many languages and backgrounds to step into English with joy, not fear. Every animal fact tucked into a verse, every musical phrase in the CD, was to entertain and empower.

Their influence has never been loud. You won't find viral videos or national awards attached to their names. But in classroom after classroom, their voices are heard—singing, chanting, guiding. They taught children how to read, yes. But more importantly, they taught them how to belong.

E.B. White achieved this in *Charlotte's Web*—writing with such respect for his audience, such clarity of purpose, the work transcends its original context to serve generations of readers. White, LaVon, and Alice wrote up to children—creating material sophisticated enough to teach while simple enough to sing along with.

Books Serving Purpose Over Profit

Sometimes the most important publishing decisions have nothing to do with sales figures or market trends. Sometimes they're about something deeper—honoring memory, preserving dignity, recognizing the sacred in the ordinary.

Some books are meant to serve. To honor. To remember. One of the most meaningful projects I've ever published came from a group of teachers in the Matanuska Valley—not writers by trade, but witnesses to a life well lived.

They came to me with a quiet request. Their colleague, a beloved teacher, was dying of a terminal illness. They had written stories—personal memories, reflections, and moments capturing the heart of a classroom, the strength of character, and the kind of impact not fading with time. What they wanted was simple: a single copy of the book, bound and finished, to give to their friend before it was too late.

I agreed without hesitation. We laid out the manuscript with the same care I'd give to any bestseller. We designed a cover. We made it beautiful. And when I told the printer what this book was—what it *meant*—they responded with something I didn't expect: they waived the printing costs and made extra copies. No invoices. Just kindness.

I matched their generosity and charged nothing for my part. It wasn't about money. It was about meaning.

This book never appeared on a bestseller list, tour festivals, or attracted reviews. But it fulfilled its purpose perfectly. It gave comfort in someone's final days. It gave voice to gratitude. It gave permanence to stories otherwise fading into silence.

Sometimes, publishing isn't about reaching the world. It's about honoring one life. And this may be the most important kind of book I've ever made.

This understanding—some things matter more than profit—connects to what all the great writers understood. Whether James creating psychologically complex characters, Tolkien building entire worlds, or Dahl refusing to lie to children about life's difficulties, they all chose purpose over easy success.

Sometimes, the most important communications serve one person perfectly rather than serving many people adequately. These purpose-driven efforts serve functions money can't measure—they honor memory, preserve dignity, and show people their lives matter."

CHAPTER NINE: QUIET STRENGTH OF EVERYDAY WRITERS

ELEMENTS OF ENDURANCE

What makes some writers last while others fade? Looking at both the historical masters and the writers I've published, several things stand out:

They tell the truth about people. Characters feel real because writers take time to understand not just what people do, but why they do it.

They respect their readers. Whether writing for children or adults, lasting writers never talk down to their audience. They trust people to handle complexity and truth.

They sound like themselves. Memorable writers have their own voice, not whatever the market demands.

They write for reasons bigger than money. Enduring work usually serves something larger—preserving culture, helping children learn, honoring memory.

They handle difficult subjects honestly. Strong writing doesn't avoid life's problems. It faces them while still offering hope.

Quiet strength of everyday writers—both historical masters and contemporary voices—lies not in volume but in conviction. They write not because they have to, but because they have something worth saying. And they say it with enough care, skill, and integrity, their words continue resonating long after the noise of their era fades away.

REFLECTION: BUILDING TO LAST

Writers you've met, from Henry James to the teachers honoring their colleague, remind us of something important: influence isn't always loud. Often, it's quiet, steady, and woven into the fabric of ordinary lives.

What foundations are you strengthening with your words?

Perhaps it's a child's sense of worth. A neighbor's trust. A friend's ability to hope again. A community's understanding of its own story.

Lasting changes often happen where no spotlights shine. In classrooms where children learn to love reading. In families where stories pass from one generation to the next. In communities where someone cares enough to preserve what otherwise might be lost.

Write as a builder. Lay quiet stones of truth, encouragement, dignity. Refuse to write down to your audience—trust them with complexity, honesty, and hope.

Your words may be the ground someone else stands on when their own strength falters.

Build to last.

Chapter Ten
Digital Tools, Timeless Truths

"We shape our tools, and thereafter our tools shape us." — Marshall McLuhan

I've watched more trends come and go than I can count—each promising to revolutionize writing, each sounding louder than the last. Somewhere along the way, it became easy to mistake the tools for the task. Writers today have apps to count their words, software to track their plots, programs to simulate their style, and platforms to measure their reach. Useful? Sometimes. Necessary? Rarely.

Great stories I've published didn't come from people obsessed with the latest technology. They came from people who still wrote in spiral-bound notebooks or typed slowly on decades-old keyboards. They weren't worried about algorithms or follower counts—they were too busy telling the truth.

Digital tools can help, yes. But they can also distract. I've seen authors delay their book for the perfect software than for lack of a story. When a tool becomes the focus, writing suffers. The voice weakens. And the author often forgets why they started in the first place.

This isn't about rejecting technology. It's about remembering what matters. No tool will give you conviction. No app will teach you to see what others overlook. And no trending format will last as long as a story told with clarity, heart, and purpose.

Tools have changed. The calling hasn't.

Your digital acts of writing carry the same responsibility as any handwritten letter or published book.

New Pathways to Readers
Alice Munro: From Small Town to Global Voice

Alice Munro started small. Stories about ordinary people in small Canadian towns. Nothing flashy. Nothing designed to grab headlines. But those quiet stories about everyday life eventually reached readers around the world and earned her a Nobel Prize.

Munro never left her small-town roots. She stayed where she was and wrote about what she knew—the people in Ontario towns, their struggles, their small victories. And the world came to her.

This matters for writers today. You don't need exotic locations or dramatic events to create meaningful work. Sometimes the most powerful stories come from paying attention to what's right in front of you: neighbors next door, conversations at the coffee shop, and family gatherings where everyone's being polite, but tensions run underneath.

Munro proved you can write about a small place and reach everywhere. Digital publishing makes this even more possible now.

I learned this lesson early in the digital transition. When eBooks first entered the conversation, most of the publishing world shrugged. Trade publications I followed spoke with confidence. eBooks were fringe. They claimed only public domain titles had made it online. Readers, they said, weren't interested. People wanted books they could hold. Digital reading was a novelty, not a movement.

In October, I parroted this view in my newsletter to writers. But by January, reality had rewritten the story. Amazon released data showing something I hadn't expected: readers were buying eBooks by the thousands. Trade publications reversed course, and so did I.

I acted quickly. A follow-up newsletter went out to our writers. I wasn't just acknowledging the shift—I was embracing it. I secured a reliable eBook conversion partner and began migrating our titles. First the bestsellers,

Chapter Ten: Digital Tools, Timeless Truths

then the backlist. I worked systematically, making sure everyone had the chance to ride the rising digital wave.

What I didn't anticipate was what followed. Readers weren't choosing between eBooks and print. Many read the digital version first, then ordered the printed book. It wasn't either-or. It was both. Digital sales led to renewed interest in printed editions, now called "p-books." Both formats began selling together, supporting each other.

Not every publisher adapted. One major distributor refused to enter the digital space. To this day, they still don't. As a result, several of their writers approached me. Though I didn't publish their print books, I converted their titles into eBooks and gave them a presence in the marketplace they otherwise wouldn't have had.

Today, nearly every title I publish launches in both formats—p-book and eBook. More and more are moving into audio. I've learned technology doesn't replace timeless storytelling. It extends it. Tools may change, but the reason we publish stays the same: to give writers a voice and readers a choice.

John Updike: Bridging High Art and Cultural Commentary

John Updike wrote everywhere. Literary magazines, mainstream publications, book reviews, even children's books. Everything got the same careful attention.

This approach—bringing quality to whatever platform you're using—matters more now than ever. Writers today move between blogs, newsletters, social media, and traditional publishing. The key is maintaining your standards across all of them.

Updike understood something crucial: your voice is your voice, whether you're writing for *The New Yorker* or a local newspaper. Don't change who you are based on where you're publishing.

Here's what reminds me of the most important shift in my own publishing practice. Technology changed the way I publish—but more importantly, it changed who could find the books I produce. Traditional methods worked well when shelves and signings were the only paths to readers. But they had limits—geography, cost, timing. Digital tools opened those doors wide.

A significant shift came when I developed our Worldwide Distribution Service. This wasn't just a new system. It was a new way to think about publishing.

Under the old model, a writer needed a warehouse, an upfront investment, and a lot of luck to keep a book available. But with the right technology in place, I flipped the equation. When a bookstore or reader places an order, my system springs into action—printing, packaging, and shipping directly to its destination. I cover the costs. I handle the logistics. The writer stays centered on writing.

A single book can now reach a reader in Anchorage, a library in Germany, a retailer in Singapore, or a bookstore in Kansas—without the writer lifting a finger.

Reach matters, but so does permanence. No title ever needs to go out of print. A book stays available as long as there's someone who wants to read it. Writers can keep copies on hand without betting on large print runs. Royalties flow with each sale, and their involvement begins and ends with cashing the check.

New technology didn't make me less personal—it made me more efficient. It leveled the field. It allowed my writers to reach readers across the world, not just across town. And it proved something I've believed from the beginning: the right tools, in the right hands, make good books go farther.

Your voice stays your voice whether you're writing a text message or a formal letter. An email to your cousin carries the same responsibility as a presentation to your boss. Social media posts deserve the same thought as newsletters. Quality travels, regardless of the platform—but only if you put it there.

Digital Challenges

Seymour Hersh: Truth-Telling in Noisy Environments

Seymour Hersh spent his career doing something simple: checking facts before printing them. While other journalists rushed to publish, Hersh

Chapter Ten: Digital Tools, Timeless Truths

took time to verify. When he exposed major scandals like My Lai and Abu Ghraib, those stories held up because he'd done the work.

In our digital age, this approach matters more than ever. Information spreads faster than truth. Anyone can publish anything. But not everyone takes responsibility for accuracy.

I learned this lesson the hard way when I was invited to contribute a story for *The Mysterious Podcast*, a nationally known series focused on strange and true events. Producers wanted something uniquely Alaskan—but it had to be factual. No legends. No speculation. Just the truth.

I accepted the challenge.

Writing a podcast script was new territory. I turned to AI—not to write the final story, but to assist with structure and research. The first draft came back polished, full of vivid scenes and gripping Bigfoot encounters in the Alaska wilderness. It read like a campfire thriller. But something sounded fishy.

Before sending it to the producers, I asked the AI a simple question: Can you verify these stories?

The answer was sobering. None of the details were true. No sources. No names. No records. Every thrilling moment had been fabricated.

This moment changed my entire approach.

From then on, I treated AI the same way I treat any reference tool: useful but never trusted without verification. I revised my prompt—no creative writing, no speculation, no folklore unless clearly identified as such. "Facts only. Verifiable sources. Traceable names." With those standards in place, I tried again.

The next draft was different. The stories it surfaced were rooted in reality—names I recognized, events I could confirm, incidents documented in public records or credible media. With this foundation, I wrote a new script. This time, it was accepted and aired.

It was well received—not because it sensationalized, but because it respected the audience. I told a true story in a world full of noise.

This experience reminded me AI is a tool—nothing more, and certainly nothing less. It can save time. It can organize. It can suggest. But it cannot be trusted blindly. Just like any draft, its output demands oversight.

In an age where misinformation travels faster than facts, my job as a publisher is to pause, verify, and stand by what I produce.

Truth still matters. But it must be pursued.

This principle shows up in the work of writers like Bill Cox, who never shouts. He doesn't chase trends or controversy. His voice—steady, thoughtful, and honest—cuts through the noise with clarity and conviction. *My Pursuit of the Axis of Evil* isn't a book about geopolitics. It's about people. Bill writes from the road, the sky, and the heart—documenting a lifetime of encounters across Siberia, Southeast Asia, India, and Alaska.

What makes Bill's work different is the way he sees. Where others carry prejudice, he brings curiosity. He took seriously the advice of the ancient traveler Pythagoras: "Check your prejudices at every port of entry." And he did—again and again, in over two dozen journeys to parts of the world most Americans only glimpse on the news.

In an age when many writers chase clicks, Bill chases connection. His voice stands out precisely because it doesn't compete. It contributes. And he continues to write, every week, in a newsletter shaped by his voice and supported by modern technology. His readers don't follow him because he shouts louder than the rest. They follow him because they trust him.

In a world where lies travel faster than truth, the person who takes time to verify becomes a guardian. When misinformation spreads instantly, your commitment to accuracy becomes a form of public service.

Anthony Trollope: Sustainable Production in Demanding Markets

Anthony Trollope wrote every morning before his day job at the postal service. He wrote consistently, daily, for years—forty-seven novels.

Trollope understood writing is work. Good work, meaningful work, but work nonetheless. You show up. You do the job. You don't wait for perfect conditions.

I see this balance in writers like Jake Jacobson, who mastered the art of consistent output without burning out. In an age built on urgency, where

Chapter Ten: Digital Tools, Timeless Truths

writers are told to post, produce, and publish without pause, Jake took a different path—one guided by rhythm, not rush. His writing emerged not from marketing calendars or productivity hacks, but from the seasons of his life in Alaska: tracking moose, guiding hunters, flying solo over mountain passes, and anchoring boats off Kodiak.

Jake wrote the way he hunted and flew—with respect, attention, and readiness. His stories are grounded in memory, not speed. Each book was built on decades of experience and told when the time felt right—not when the market demanded it. And yet, over time, the output became astonishing: more than a dozen titles capturing the humor, hardship, and heart of Alaska's interior and coast.

He writes consistently, but never carelessly. Every chapter carries the weight of firsthand knowledge—whether he's describing a near-death landing in a sudden squall or laughing through a hunting mishap with a client who packed sardines but forgot bullets. Jake doesn't invent stories. He lived them. He still does.

Jake Jacobson is proof; sustainable writing isn't about doing more. It's about doing it right—and doing it long enough so the work stands when the hurry fades.

But sustainability also means staying connected. Writers today are under constant pressure to produce—more books, more posts, more visibility. Demands come from all sides: readers who want the next installment, platforms rewarding daily content, and an industry often confusing noise with value.

Mary Ann Poll sets the standard for balancing these demands. I tell writers all the time: if you want to see what steady, meaningful engagement looks like, look to Mary Ann. She's not just a writer—she's active. She's a charter member of Author Masterminds and participates in the Readers and Writers Book Club. She posts consistently. She shows up for interviews, contributes to discussions, and responds to readers. She doesn't disappear between books.

Mary Ann maintains a podcast, *Real Ghost Chatter*, where she discusses supernatural themes and connects her audience to the topics she cares about. She shares behind-the-scenes insights and personal reflections, always staying within the bounds of truth. Her updates are frequent, but never frantic. She doesn't flood the feed. She adds value.

And she writes. With care. With purpose. She doesn't sacrifice the quality of her books just to stay visible. She keeps both the writing and the outreach moving—side by side, not in competition.

Good communication is work—meaningful work, but work nonetheless. You show up, do the job, and don't wait for perfect conditions. Sustainable communication comes from treating it like the important work it is.

DIGITAL-AGE STORYTELLING

Italo Calvino: Forms for Fragmented Times

Italo Calvino wrote stories you could read in any order. His books didn't follow straight lines. Readers could jump around, start in the middle, skip chapters—and still get the full experience.

This approach works well in our digital world, where people's attention jumps between screens, notifications, and platforms. Sometimes writers need to accommodate how people read today, not how we wish they read.

This understanding shows up in a most successful book. In a time when attention is split across screens, alerts, and endless scrolling, *Eddie the Ermine* proves something simple and powerful: you don't need more pages to make a lasting impression—you need purpose on every page.

Josh Verhagen understood this from the beginning. He wrote a short story. He created a thoughtful experience. *Eddie the Ermine* delivers a complete narrative in just a few pages—clear, direct, engaging, and visually rich. A young ermine learns not to take what isn't his and discovers the reward of doing something hard. The lesson lands, not through explanation, but through example.

Brilliance of the book lies in its restraint. Illustrations do more than decorate—they teach. Every page invites interaction. Hidden animals draw the reader's eye. Local Alaskan scenery grounds the story in a real place.

And at the end, a few carefully chosen pages of wildlife facts turn a quick read into an educational tool.

Children love to revisit it, and parents appreciate both its brevity and its message. It holds a young reader's attention without demanding it, and it respects the adult reading it aloud, knowing their time is also precious.

Eddie the Ermine works because it doesn't try to do everything. It does one thing well—and enough. In publishing, a lesson worth remembering. Sometimes, less isn't just more. It's exactly what's needed.

ROBERT LOUIS STEVENSON: ECONOMY AS LITERARY VIRTUE

Robert Louis Stevenson wrote short, tight stories. *Dr. Jekyll and Mr. Hyde* is barely 25,000 words, but it's lasted more than a century. He didn't pad his work. Every word had a purpose.

In our age of short attention spans, there's wisdom in Stevenson's approach. Sometimes the most powerful message comes in the smallest package.

This principle—new formats can serve traditional values—appears in some of my most innovative recent work. Victoria Hardesty and Nancy Perez didn't set out to reinvent storytelling. They set out to honor it. Their *Wonder Horse* series tells classic, heartfelt stories—young people, beloved horses, real challenges, and the deep bond forged between them. These are the kinds of books readers pass down. But their creation was anything but old-fashioned.

Living miles apart, both dealing with serious health issues, Victoria and Nancy wrote together using tools their childhood selves could never have imagined: email, internet research, and hours of phone calls. Technology made the work possible. Values behind the stories made it matter.

What worked wasn't just how they used digital tools—it was why. They leaned on truth. Every book in the series draws from decades of firsthand experience with Arabian horses. Details are accurate, the struggles are grounded, and the settings—while shaped by narrative—are rooted in a world they lived.

Victoria brought the technical knowledge. Nancy brought storytelling instincts shaped by years in advertising and a lifetime of close friendship.

Together, they turned new tools into a bridge—not a shortcut. They used the internet not for trends but for depth. Their goal wasn't to chase attention—it was to tell stories worth reading.

And they succeeded. The *Wonder Horse* series earned its place quietly, through quality, character, and care. These books are available on every major platform—print and digital—but the heart remains unchanged. These are traditional stories, told with integrity, built using modern tools. Proof the format may evolve, but the values never need to.

In our age of scattered attention, the strongest message comes in the smallest package. Economy serves clarity—when you say exactly what needs saying and nothing more. Economical uses of digital tools often carry more weight than longer communications.

Publisher's Digital Toolkit

In a world where screens glow with countless messages and algorithms reward speed over substance, the principles guiding meaningful publishing remain unchanged. The digital revolution has given me new tools, but my true power still comes from the same source—empowering writers to find their voice and readers to find their choice.

Digital publishing didn't just change how I make books—it changed which books I choose to make.

Twenty years ago, a manuscript needed broad market appeal, strong sales projections, and a budget justifying a large print run. I had to ask: Can this book sell fast and in volume? Because if it couldn't, the risk was too high.

Today, I ask a different question: Can this book reach the right reader?

Technology made this shift possible—and practical. With print-on-demand, I no longer gamble on inventory. A single copy gets printed when someone orders it. No storage. No spoilage. No pallets of unsold books. A title selling a few hundred copies over its lifetime can still be worth producing.

Digital distribution widened the gate even further. I don't need to negotiate shelf space or rely on physical bookstores to move copies. A regional memoir, a hyper-niche history, or a specialized how-to guide can find its readers through Amazon, Ingram, or direct-to-consumer platforms—anywhere in the world.

Production costs dropped, too. Professional formatting, typesetting, and design can be done faster and more affordably than ever before. I can take on smaller projects because the tools to shape them have become more efficient and accessible.

Marketing changed most of all. Broad-market advertising once ate entire budgets. Now, I can reach readers directly—through newsletters, podcasts, blogs, Facebook groups, and targeted online communities. A niche audience doesn't need to be big—it needs to be reachable. And digital tools make this happen.

I use data now. I can study trends, test interest, and respond to signals—before a book even goes to press. I can support long-tail publishing, where titles don't sell thousands overnight but keep selling for years. Books once dismissed as "too small" are now proving their worth over time.

I still care about quality. This hasn't changed. But digital publishing lets me champion stories deserving to be told—even when they don't fit old models. It lets me say yes more often. And it's helping more writers find their audience—not by shouting louder, but by going where the listeners already are.

But through all these changes, I've held to the basics—honesty, fairness, and long-term commitment. Some call this old-school. I call it the standard. And sticking to it has made all the difference.

I've watched the digital age reshape publishing—faster production, wider distribution, new marketing tools. I embraced the technology. But I never let it replace the principles. I still pick up the phone. I still honor every agreement. I still tell writers the truth, even when it's not what they want to hear. And I don't make promises I can't keep.

This is not just good business—it's the foundation of trust.

It's why I was honored to receive the Better Business Bureau Torch Award. Recognition wasn't for flashy innovation. It was for doing business the right way—consistently, transparently, and with integrity. The Torch Award confirmed what I've believed all along: character counts, and people notice.

This approach has carried me through. It's why I'm able to publish books other houses won't touch—memoirs with modest reach, local histories, personal essays, regional guides. Technology makes those books possible. My values make them sustainable. I support the work, but more importantly, I support the writer.

When others turned to automation, I turned to community. How the Readers and Writers Book Club and Author Masterminds were born—not out of trend, but out of mission. Those programs aren't quick fixes. They're long-term investments in real people.

And here's the difference. Technology helps. But trust builds careers. Tools have changed. My principles haven't. And in the long run, what matters most.

Your digital-age writing gains power not through viral tactics or keyword optimization, but through commitment to truth told with clarity and compassion. In a landscape built for distraction, your attention becomes a revolutionary act. In spaces rewarding conformity, your authentic voice offers essential contrast. In platforms promoting reaction over reflection, your thoughtful perspective provides rare wisdom.

Write for people, not algorithms. Create for understanding, not metrics. Speak from conviction, not calculation.

The most important digital skill isn't technical mastery but spiritual discernment—knowing when to connect and when to disconnect, when to speak and when to listen, when to publish and when to protect developing work from premature exposure.

Reflection: Using Tools to Serve Truth

Technology changes. Responsibility doesn't.

Every email you send, every post you share, every digital word you write carries the same moral weight as any handwritten letter or published book.

The question isn't whether you should embrace new tools—it's how you'll use them to serve what matters most.

Will your digital presence build up or tear down? Will your online words create connection or division? Will your use of technology honor truth or chase trends?

Chapter Ten: Digital Tools, Timeless Truths

Writers who adapt to new tools while maintaining their integrity don't just survive change—they use it to extend their reach and deepen their impact.

Your voice matters in the digital age, not because it's the loudest, but because it's trustworthy. Not because it follows every trend, but because it serves timeless principles.

Use the tools. But let the truth use you.

Chapter Eleven
Enduring Legacy of Writers

"Hope is not a prognostication—it's an orientation of the spirit."
— Václav Havel

After exploring how writers use new tools while holding to timeless truths, we arrive at the deepest question of all: What makes certain words outlive their creators? What separates the books still being read decades later from those forgotten by next season?

Every age produces an ocean of words—millions of pages written, spoken, posted, and forgotten. Yet some sentences remain. They rise above their moment and continue speaking long after their writers have passed, not because they were louder, but because they were truer.

I've learned the difference between popular and lasting isn't always obvious at first. Some books launch with fanfare and fade quickly. Others start quietly and keep growing, finding new readers year after year. Words with staying power share certain qualities—not flashy ones, but fundamental ones.

This is about writers who understood their job wasn't to chase applause but to plant seeds. To write not just for their moment but for moments they'd never see. To trust their vision when others didn't understand it, and to keep faith with readers who hadn't been born yet.

I've been privileged to work with writers like this—who cared more about impact than immediate success, who built their work to last rather than to sell fast. Their examples, alongside the great writers who came before them, teach us what it means to leave a legacy.

Writing for Unknown Readers
Madeleine L'Engle: Faith in Future Audiences

When Madeleine L'Engle faced over thirty rejections for *A Wrinkle in Time*, she continued revising and submitting the manuscript despite having no guarantee it would ever find its audience. This persistence came from knowing her words would eventually find their proper readers, even if the path proved longer and more twisting than the writer might wish.

L'Engle's approach to writing was fundamentally optimistic without being naive. She understood the publishing industry's commercial realities and faced them squarely, but she held what she called "the obligation to keep on doing the thing you're meant to do." This balanced perspective—facing current limitations while maintaining faith in future possibilities—offers valuable guidance for writers in today's rapidly changing communication landscapes.

Unlike writers who wrote for immediate recognition or market success, L'Engle kept a longer view of literary significance. "You have to write the book wanting to be written," she advised. "And if the book will be too difficult for grown-ups, then you write it for children." This willingness to trust unknown future readers rather than targeting only established markets fueled work continuing to find new audiences for nearly sixty years.

I saw this same faith in future readers when Sara Donkersloot brought me *Down by the River*. At first glance, I saw a beautifully written children's book—gentle rhythm, regional wildlife, and stunning illustrations by Dale Preston. It had all the marks of a solid Alaska-themed picture book. What I didn't yet see was its long-term impact.

Then came later.

Battle of the Books selected *Down by the River*, and almost overnight, I received an order for more than 3,000 copies. A single inclusion opened the door to hundreds of classrooms and school libraries across the state. The book was successful. Teachers used it, students remembered it, and communities embraced it.

Years later, the same happened with *Out on the Tundra*. Different book. Same result. Combination of lyrical language, Alaska-native animals, and Dale's signature artwork proved a winning formula again.

And then it stopped—not because the books lost value, but because the creative team couldn't continue. Dale's passing brought the series to a quiet end. His illustrations weren't just visual—they were vital. They captured something unique, and replacing them would've changed the heart of the work. Sara stepped away, and the series paused where it stood.

But the books themselves haven't faded. They're still in classrooms. Still in libraries. Still on shelves across Alaska. They were ahead of their time in one simple way: they were built to last.

I stood by these books even before their inclusion in Battle of the Books. I believed in their purpose, their message, and their quiet power to teach without preaching. Belief paid off—not as a short-term hit, but as a long-term contribution to Alaskan education and culture.

Sometimes legacy isn't loud. It's a book still being read years after its release. It's a child who can name ten Alaskan animals because of one rhyme. It's a classroom sharing a story over winter break, or a school in a bush village finding a piece of home in the pages.

Like L'Engle, Sara understood the difference between writing for immediate success and writing for lasting impact. Both writers showed faith in readers they'd never meet, trusting their work would find its way to the people who needed it most.

You might be writing for someone who desperately needs what you have to say—they just haven't found it yet.

W.B. YEATS: CONTINUOUS REINVENTION

Throughout his long literary career spanning the late 19th century through the early 20th century, W.B. Yeats continuously reinvented his poetic voice and thematic concerns—moving from romantic Celtic mythology to modernist political engagement to philosophical exploration of cyclical history to stark confrontation with mortality. This evolution across changing literary and historical contexts shows writers how artistic growth—rather than clinging to a static style—often shapes lasting literary value.

Yeats's earliest poetry emerged from the Celtic Revival movement seeking to establish distinctive Irish cultural identity through engagement with mythology and folklore. Rather than remaining within this successful early style, Yeats repeatedly challenged both his readers' expectations and his own established patterns. His middle period engaged directly with Irish political struggle and revolutionary violence, while his later work explored abstract philosophical systems and unflinching confrontation with aging.

Unlike writers who maintain a consistent recognizable approach throughout their careers, Yeats willingly risked alienating existing audiences through artistic evolution rather than repetition. This willingness to grow and change explains his ongoing literary significance across changing contexts.

I've seen this kind of evolution in Mike Dillingham. Some writers keep writing the same book over and over. Mike didn't.

He started with *Rivers: Diary of a Blind Alaska Racing Sled Dog*, a heartfelt story inspired by a real dog and a real bond. At first, it was simple—Mike loved dogs, especially Rivers. The idea of a blind sled dog competing in races wasn't just a story idea. It was a purpose. And when the first book went out into the world, people—especially children—responded. They bought the book. They believed in it.

Mike leaned into this response. He visited schools, signed copies, and told stories. And what began as one book became three. But it wasn't just a trilogy—it was a transformation.

Mike grew as a writer with each new title. He listened to kids' questions, watched their faces as they met Rivers in person, and slowly began to shift his storytelling. His later books tackled bigger themes: grief, loyalty, courage, even social challenges like disability and abandonment. The books stayed fun, but they carried more weight. They weren't just about racing anymore. They were about life—seen through the eyes of a blind dog who kept moving forward.

And then, the real Rivers passed away.

This moment changed everything. Sales dropped. School visits became harder. And for Mike, the joy from sharing the book faded. Rivers wasn't just the inspiration—he was the heartbeat of the project. Without him, something essential was gone.

Mike stayed in touch. He still writes. He still reflects. And the evolution started with a story about one dog became a life built on connection—with readers, with animals, with Alaska.

Both Yeats and Mike understood the same truth: lasting writers don't just repeat what worked before. They grow with their experiences, even when it means leaving comfortable territory behind. Willingness to change and evolve often creates more lasting impact than sticking rigidly to one approach.

CHARACTER AS FOUNDATION
Edna Ferber: People Who Feel Real

While literary styles and cultural contexts continually evolve, Edna Ferber's career demonstrates the enduring centrality of character to meaningful storytelling across changing landscapes. Her novels and plays spanning the early to mid-twentieth century remain engaging because she created complex, fully realized characters whose humanity rises above historical circumstances.

Ferber's most lasting works, like *So Big* and *Giant,* built their narratives around protagonists embodying both timeless qualities and specific cultural moments. Her characters face particular circumstances of their era but embody universal qualities of resilience, creativity, and moral integrity recognizable to readers in any time period.

Unlike writers pinpointing primarily on plot or theme, Ferber developed narratives emerging organically from her characters' particular personalities, values, and circumstances. This character-centered approach creates stories feeling authentic rather than artificially constructed across changing literary fashions.

This emphasis on character-driven storytelling reminds me of Marianne Schlegelmilch and her books. Her stories are deeply rooted in the emotional and psychological lives of her characters. They don't just inhabit Alaska; they breathe it, respond to it, and are shaped by its beauty and hardship.

Feather from a Stranger or *Acts of Kindness*—these books are built around characters who feel as familiar and textured as neighbors. Marianne doesn't simply place people in a plot; she lets the people *be* the plot. Their motivations, fears, and quiet triumphs drive the story forward. They don't need spectacle to be memorable—just honesty.

What makes her characters resonate is how they reflect real complexity: resilience laced with doubt, kindness shadowed by pain, and a deep yearning for connection. Her background as a nurse often informs her sensitivity to emotional undercurrents, and it shows.

Ferber achieved much of her character development through precise, revealing dialogue reflecting both individual personality and cultural context. This attention to how people express themselves rather than how literary convention suggests they should creates characters continuing to feel alive and authentic despite changing linguistic patterns.

Both Ferber and Marianne understood the same principle: readers remember people, not plots. When you capture what makes people human—flawed, complex, still fighting—they stay with readers long after facts are forgotten.

Émile Zola: Truth as North Star

Throughout his literary career amid rapidly changing cultural and political circumstances in 19th-century France, Émile Zola maintained his commitment to social truth regardless of personal consequences. His willingness to confront powerful institutions and popular prejudices through both fiction and journalism demonstrates how writing guided by principled truth-seeking rather than self-protection can achieve lasting significance beyond immediate reception.

Zola's literary approach, established through his Rougon-Macquart cycle—twenty novels exploring how heredity and environment shape character and destiny—reflected his commitment to unflinching examination of social reality. Unlike romanticized literature of his era, Zola portrayed poverty, alcoholism, labor exploitation, and class conflict with documentary precision informed by extensive research.

Unlike writers chasing acclaim or commercial success, Zola risked his reputation and safety to stand on principle. His famous open letter *J'Accuse...!* exposed antisemitic persecution during the Dreyfus Affair and cost him a conviction for libel and temporary exile from France. His willingness to face personal consequences in defense of truth shows how

Chapter Eleven: Enduring Legacy of Writers

writing anchored in moral conviction, not self-interest, often carries enduring weight far beyond literary recognition.

This commitment to truth above personal interest reminds me of Weston Fields. Some writers write to ride the wave. Weston wrote to preserve what could have been lost.

When I first met him, Weston looked every bit the Kodiak fisherman—rubber boots, suspenders, wool shirt. He was there to support his mother, who had written a book about ranching history on the island. She spoke first. He said almost nothing. When he finally did, it was to tell me—gently—he had already edited her manuscript. I chuckled to myself. He didn't look like any editor I'd ever met.

Turns out, I was the one who needed editing.

Weston wasn't just an editor. He was a scholar, a linguist, and a historian with a mind like a steel trap and a heart to match. He spoke five languages fluently. He had interviewed every living figure associated with the Dead Sea Scrolls. He served as Executive Director of the Dead Sea Scrolls Foundation. And though his roots were in Kodiak, his reach extended across the globe—right into the caves of Qumran, the offices of scholars, and the courts of Middle Eastern royalty.

He believed the story of the Dead Sea Scrolls—the documents, the discovery, the drama—had to be told. Not just as a timeline, but as a record of what nearly went wrong. He documented how for decades, much of the Scrolls' content was hidden away, controlled by a small group of scholars. He fought for access, for fairness, and for accuracy. And through it all, he did the slow, careful work of gathering facts, cross-checking sources, and building trust.

I saw this firsthand. More than once, as we worked on *The Dead Sea Scrolls: A Full History*, he paused mid-conversation to confirm a detail. Not online. Not from a book. But from a prince—on his speed dial. Fluent Arabic, calm tone, quiet certainty. Then back to work.

Weston wrote from deep conviction. He never asked, "Will this sell?" He asked, "Is this true?" And he built something lasting, not because it was trendy, but because it was necessary. Volume One of his history remains the most comprehensive narrative of the Scrolls' journey from cave to public access. He died before he finished the later volumes. But he lived to change the field.

Like Zola, Weston protected ancient truth. He honored it—with scholarship, with stewardship, and with the kind of quiet integrity not needing marketing. It just needs time. Serving truth is more important than keeping peace.

MEMORY AND TRANSFORMATION

Marcel Proust: Making Meaning from Experience

When Marcel Proust devoted the last 14 years of his life to creating his massive novel *In Search of Lost Time*, he demonstrated extraordinary commitment to exploring a single essential question: how memory shapes consciousness and creates meaning from temporal experience. This monumental project—roughly 1.2 million words developed while confined to a cork-lined bedroom due to illness—stands as a powerful example of how artistic exploration of core experience can achieve lasting literary impact.

Proust's literary approach centered on meticulous examination of how sensory experiences—especially involuntary memories triggered by taste, smell, or sound—illuminate connections between past and present consciousness. His famous madeleine scene doesn't just describe remembering but re-experiencing past moments with greater clarity and significance than during their original occurrence.

Unlike writers focused on external events or social observation, Proust turned his attention inward to examine consciousness itself with unprecedented precision and detail. This concentration on consciousness as a legitimate subject for extended artistic exploration established psychological interiority as a central concern of modern literature.

This approach—transforming personal experience into universal insight—shows up in one of the most powerful books I've published. Some books come from a place so raw they feel like an open wound turned into a lifeline. *The Truth About Suicide* is one of those books.

Dr. Deb Wood wasn't trying to build a platform. She was trying to save lives.

Out in Talkeetna, she had built something rare—a retreat for veterans using sled dogs as therapy animals, trained by the veterans themselves. It was hands-on. Real. Rooted in the land and in trust. The idea was simple: give the veterans purpose, responsibility, and a bond with a responding and nonjudgmental creature. And it worked. For a while.

But not for everyone.

Despite all the success stories, there were still losses. Suicides. Men and women who had come home but couldn't find peace—couldn't outpace the pain. When suicide happened, Deb said, "I have to write this book." And she did. Not for recognition. For them.

The Truth About Suicide became her answer to those tragedies. A blend of science, testimony, and deep compassion, the book dismantles myths, speaks frankly about trauma, and offers a path forward. It doesn't preach. It reaches. It holds a mirror up to the reader, then holds out a hand.

And the place behind the book? I visited. A 640-acre property wrapped in quiet Alaska forest. Mt. Denali rising in the distance. Cabins tucked among the trees. An upper room in the main house where, if you just stood still, you could almost feel the healing happen. The retreat wasn't flashy. It was sacred. Built with intention. Carved from personal pain into collective possibility.

Some writers write what sells. Deb wrote what saved. Like Proust, she understood how personal experience, when examined deeply and honestly, can illuminate universal truths about the human condition.

WILLIAM SHAKESPEARE: CREATING THROUGH COMMUNITY

While often celebrated as an individual genius, Shakespeare's enduring impact emerged from a deeply collaborative process. His plays were shaped through interaction with actors, fellow writers, audiences, and source materials—demonstrating lasting literary significance often comes through engagement with community rather than isolation.

Shakespeare's creative genius lay not in inventing wholly original stories but in transforming existing materials—historical accounts, folk tales, and earlier plays—into works of extraordinary depth and resonance. His ability to create works functioning simultaneously as popular entertainment and profound literary experiences shows how enduring significance can emerge when writers engage deeply with their audiences and traditions.

This collaborative approach reminds me of one of my most successful publishing partnerships. Some books begin with a single voice. Others rise from a multitude of lived experiences. *The Day Trees Bent to the Ground* was born from both—a determined teacher, a seasoned photographer, and a community shaken by Alaska's most powerful earthquake. Together, they made something no one person could have achieved alone.

It started when Janet Boylan, retired from decades of teaching, took up bridge and tennis at the Anchorage Senior Center. Faced with budget shortfalls, she set her sights on a project to raise funds and preserve history at the same time. Her idea? Gather personal stories from those who survived the 1964 earthquake and print them in a small, self-made booklet.

Then Dolores Roguszka entered the story.

Dolores had been a writer and professional photographer for more than fifty years. She had submitted articles and photographs to dozens of magazines, taught photography at UCLA, and even published a guidebook for Amphoto. She'd never intended to do another book. But when she read Jan's call for stories in the Senior Center newsletter, she dusted off an old, unpublished article—one she'd written right after the quake—and picked up the phone.

They clicked immediately. They wanted something worthy of the moment—something honoring history and helping the Senior Center at the same time.

Then they found their way to my office.

I didn't just agree to publish the book. I got involved. I guided the manuscript, discussed print quantities, and supported their mission from the very first meeting. When the book was printed—when Jan and Dolores held those first copies in their hands—it wasn't just their victory. It was a shared triumph.

Chapter Eleven: Enduring Legacy of Writers

One hundred and fifty firsthand accounts. People thrown down hallways. Drinks spilled in laps. Loved ones lost—and found. A baby tossed to safety in a snowbank. Each voice captured with care, edited with respect, and preserved for generations. *The Day Trees Bent to the Ground* sold well. It's now in its sixth printing. And more than $40,000 in royalties has gone directly to the Anchorage Senior Center.

Like Shakespeare, Jan and Dolores understood great work often comes from collaboration—bringing together different skills, perspectives, and experiences to create something larger than any individual contribution—each contributing their piece to something larger than any individual could create alone.

WHAT REALLY LASTS

Looking back over decades of publishing, I've learned the difference between popular and lasting isn't always obvious at first. Some books launch with fanfare and fade quickly. Others start quietly and keep growing.

When Dwaine Schuldt brought me Lt. Henry Tureman Allen's 1885 expedition journal, it didn't look like a bestseller. At first glance, it looked like a dry, historical report—more academic than commercial. I wasn't even sure it was legal to publish.

But Dwaine kept showing up. He'd stop by my booth at the Christmas bazaar, asking smart questions about publishing. Always friendly. Always engaged. At first, I thought he was just curious. Later, I realized he had something in mind.

Dwaine believed the story deserved to be told. Not as fiction. Not as a rewritten adventure. But exactly as Allen had written it. A firsthand account of Alaska as it was in the 1800s. A time when miners and trappers failed to return because they treated Native Alaskans with arrogance or suspicion. Allen's party survived by doing the opposite—by listening, following Native trails, and sharing meals with the people who had already lived in the region for 10,000 years.

Eventually, I said yes. Not because of market trends. Because of Dwaine's conviction.

It became one of our best sellers. It found its place at signings, in schools, with readers who wanted real history told by someone who had walked the land. Dwaine poured himself into promoting it—showing up at events, talking to readers, sharing the story. And it worked.

Sadly, Dwaine passed away after a battle with cancer. Sales slowed, sure. But readers still find it. Because the story still matters.

Another book proving lasting value over time is Ann D. Roberts' *Alaska Gardening Guide*. This isn't a coffee table book for casual glancing. It's dog-eared and soil-smudged. It lives in greenhouses, on porches, and at the elbow of anyone who's tried to make something grow in northern soil.

My wife Lois has been using her copy for more than two decades—and if it ever goes missing, we're in trouble. This guide doesn't offer broad theory or idealized climates. It deals with what Alaskans face: short seasons, cold soil, heavy rain, and growing zones, making most seed packets useless.

I've had people tell me they never thought they could grow anything until they opened Ann's book. Teachers use it. Clubs share it. Families pass it down. In an age of instant information and digital distractions, here's a book standing like a sturdy trellis—supporting not just vegetables, but people. People trying to live closer to the land. Trying to feed their families. Trying to make life work in cold, hard places.

Why will this book still matter in fifty years? Because good food still matters. Self-reliance still matters. And truth—especially truth grows—never goes out of print.

Warren Troy surprised me by moving in a completely different direction from his wilderness memoirs to children's literature. His *Mike in the Woods* isn't just a new book. It was a new direction. A children's story, told with gentleness and wonder, about a young boy who wanders into the woods and finds an unexpected guide—a bear who doesn't frighten, but teaches.

Warren distilled his wilderness wisdom into a format children could understand. *Mike in the Woods* isn't a departure from his values—it's a translation of them. It holds the same respect for nature, the same quiet pacing, the same sense of awe.

Chapter Eleven: Enduring Legacy of Writers

The shift surprised me—and it worked. Warren wrote not just to tell a story, but to pass something down. A love for nature. A reverence for wild spaces. Believing the woods still have something to say, especially to the youngest among us.

And the most honest books create the most lasting impact. This book made me realize the power of honest storytelling was *The Bears of Manley* by Sarkis Atamian.

Sarkis came to me with a 220,000-word manuscript. What made me pause was the subject: a hunter's life in the Alaskan wilderness, written not just as an adventure, but as a deep exploration of what it means to hunt—ethically, spiritually, and psychologically.

Sarkis had something he needed to say—about hunting, about manhood, about truth. And he said it with clarity, depth, and unapologetic conviction.

He didn't sugarcoat the reality. He knew people would challenge the ethics of hunting. He knew activists would criticize him. But he also knew the story mattered. Not just the blood and grit of the hunt, but the solitude, the preparation, the reverence, the humility before the wild. This wasn't a trophy tale. It was a philosophical memoir.

His honesty wasn't harsh—it was necessary. And it's the reason his work still finds readers who are looking for something real.

Legacy Lesson

After decades in publishing—watching thousands of manuscripts pass across my desk—I've come to believe one simple truth: the words last aren't always the ones launching with a splash. They're not always trendy or loud. More often than not, they're quiet. Steady. True.

They're the ones sitting with people long after the cover is closed.

A popular book may generate buzz. It may catch attention with a clever hook or flashy campaign. But a lasting book doesn't need flash. It needs substance. A clear voice. A real heart. It needs to tell the truth in a way resonating across seasons and generations.

I've seen it firsthand: the difference between what sells fast and what stays meaningful. Enduring books are the ones showing up years later in a well-used copy—highlighted, dog-eared, handed from parent to child.

They show up in letters, in quiet thank-you notes, in readers who say, "the book helped me get through something." They're the ones people don't forget.

Lasting books aren't always bestsellers. But they're lifelines. They become companions. And they change people—not all at once, but over time. They change the way someone sees the world. Or forgives someone. Or decides to write a letter, make a call, plant a seed.

Trends fade. Impact endures.

The lesson publishing has taught me again and again. The worth of a story isn't measured only in units sold. It's measured in people reached. Hearts touched. Lives quietly shifted because someone sat down, opened a book, and saw something of themselves—and something more.

Writers who understand this—who write not for immediate applause but for lasting connection—create the kind of work outliving its creators. They join the long line of writers who've shaped the world not through volume but through truth, not through noise but through clarity, not through speed but through staying power.

These are the writers worth remembering. And worth becoming.

REFLECTION: BECOMING PART OF THE NEVER-ENDING STORY

Writers you've traveled with throughout this journey remind us: Words outlive their creators.

Long after voices fall silent, pages whisper. Stories carry. Truth persists.

Each sentence written with moral purpose becomes a stone in a path others can follow—centuries later.

Now, you stand in the same tradition.

You are not writing into a void. You are weaving your words into a living tapestry beginning before you and stretching far beyond you.

Your acts of courage, your careful truths, your unseen kindnesses—they matter more than you know.

Some reader, someday, may gather strength from a story you leave behind. Some weary soul may find light in a letter you thought was forgotten. Some quiet moment you capture may ripple outward in ways you'll never witness.

Chapter Eleven: Enduring Legacy of Writers

You don't need certainty to write with faith.

You only need to believe truth, once spoken with love and clarity, finds its way.

So write.

Write knowing you are part of something larger, older, and stronger than any passing storm.

Write because your words may be someone else's beginning.

And in doing so, you become part of the enduring legacy of writers—the long, unbroken line of those who dared to shape the world with nothing but their pens and their hope.

Chapter Twelve
Writers Who Changed the World for the Better

"Words—so innocent and powerless as they are, as standing in a dictionary, how potent for good and evil they become in the hands of one who knows how to combine them." — Nathaniel Hawthorne

After walking with writers who shaped history, the journey turns inward. This chapter is not about what others wrote. It's about what you will write. The torch passes not to the next celebrated name, but to you—now carrying the clarity, courage, and calling these writers once shouldered alone.

Words don't vanish. They reverberate.

They resonate in the hush after a stirring speech. In the silence following a well-chosen phrase. In the stillness of a soul just moved by a line of prose.

You've spent these chapters walking beside writers who wrote through noise, war, rejection, silence, and censorship—writers who dared to believe even one voice, raised in truth, might shift the world's direction by a single, essential degree.

But their stories are not meant to be admired from behind the glass of history. They're meant to be continued.

The task is now yours.

Sacred Responsibility

What Writers Must Understand

Writing isn't a hobby. It isn't therapy. It isn't something to do just because you've got a little free time and a story bouncing around in your head. Writing, at its core, is stewardship. Writers take ideas—raw, wild, dangerous ideas—and shape them into words someone else might carry for the rest of their life.

This isn't a burden. It's a privilege.

As a writer you need to understand—someone out there is going to believe you! Someone will take your words as truth. They might not remember your name. They may never quote your book. But they'll carry a piece of what you've written into their relationships, their decisions, their understanding of the world.

And this means your work matters. Even if you don't sell many copies. Even if you never win an award. Even if your book ends up in a secondhand store someday with a cracked spine and a coffee stain across the back cover.

Your work still matters.

Write like it does. Write like someone's future depends on it. Because, in a way, it does.

Write with intention. Write with clarity. Write with kindness. And never forget—writers shape the world readers will live in tomorrow.

Hard Truth About Integrity

Over the years, I've read more manuscripts than I can count—each one carrying its writer's hopes, fears, and often, deeply held convictions. One in particular stands out.

Courtney Larsen wrote a book confronting a pressing social issue. His concern wasn't misplaced. He believed the legal system had begun not just interpreting law, but creating it—and in the process, had started to shift the cultural and moral ground under our feet. His words reflected a real urgency. He wasn't writing for attention. He was writing because he believed people needed to understand what was happening.

Trouble was, his passion had hardened into confrontation. The tone of the book was so sharp, so unyielding, even those who shared his viewpoint would hesitate to stand beside it. I told him the truth—not to discourage, but to redirect. I said, "You're trying to raise awareness, but you're building a wall instead."

I suggested a different path. Use public facts. Quote court cases, legal decisions, respected news articles—let those speak for themselves. Don't tell readers what to think. Show them what's happening, and let them decide. This way, you're not hammering a message. You're offering a light.

He was reluctant at first, but he listened. He came to see books with impact, don't shout. They guide. They give the reader room to reason, to reflect, to agree in their own time and their own words. The strongest voices in publishing aren't always the loudest. They're the ones leading with clarity, not force—and trust their readers to arrive with them.

This kind of writing people remember doesn't just win arguments. It changes minds.

SUCCESS VERSUS SIGNIFICANCE
The Choice All Writers Make

When Suzanne Bassette walked through my office door with *Talkeetna Twines*, she carried more than a manuscript—she brought a piece of her life. She didn't use her real name, but everything else about her was honest. An Air Force officer, a nurse, a woman who had lived deep in Alaska's backcountry—Suzanne had earned every sentence she'd written.

Her manuscript was strong. Clean. Confident. Wilderness scenes rang true. Her characters were believable, especially Rebecca, the protagonist who fled violence and sought healing in Alaska's raw, unforgiving land.

But there was one misfit scene. A graphic sexual encounter, written in detail, clashing with the tone of the rest of the book. It felt like someone else had written it. After reading it, I called Suzanne and asked her to come in.

When she sat down across from me, I didn't start with critique. I started with a question.

"Suzanne, how well do you know your character, Rebecca?"

She answered without hesitation. "I know her very well."

"Then help me know her, too. Write out a full character profile—where she grew up, what her parents were like, her earliest memories, her relationships, her scars. Everything. I want to see the woman behind the words."

She returned a few days later with a character profile reading like a dossier. It was detailed, thoughtful, and intimate. As I read through it, I realized Rebecca wasn't just a character—she was a reflection of Suzanne's strength and restraint, her survival and resilience.

I called Suzanne back into the office.

"After reading this," I said, tapping the file, "let me ask again: does Rebecca—your Rebecca—do what you wrote in the scene?"

Suzanne paused. She looked down. Then she quietly said, "No. I know she wouldn't."

I nodded. "Then why did you write it this way?"

Her answer was honest—and heartbreaking.

"Because I've heard you need something like this if you want your book to sell."

I don't recall every word I said next, but I remember the feeling. It wasn't judgment—it was sadness. I reminded her of something I tell writers who sit across from me: don't write for the algorithm, the critic, or the trend. Write for your reader. Write for the person who'll carry your words long after you're gone.

She went home and rewrote the scene. When she brought the new version in, it was everything the original lacked. Intimate, yes—but not exploitative. Romantic, not graphic. Rebecca's dignity remained intact, and the story was stronger for it.

Months later, after the book was published, Suzanne emailed me.

"Thank you," she wrote. "I sent a copy of *Talkeetna Twines* to my father."

She told me his response: He had written back to say how much he appreciated and enjoyed it. "One of the things I really liked," he told her, "Was, it didn't have all sexual stuff."

Then Suzanne said something to me I've never forgotten: "Evan, I now realize—if I had left the scene in, I couldn't have sent a copy of the book to my father."

Chapter Twelve: Writers Who Changed the World for the Better

This stayed with me. And it still reminds me why telling the truth in your story—and staying true to your characters—matters more than following trends. Suzanne chose to pull her story back in line with her character—and in doing so, she honored her voice, her family, and her readers.

It's easy to write what sells. Harder to write what matters.

But when writers choose integrity over impulse, they don't just create better stories—they create work lasting.

WRITERS WHO UNDERSTOOD THEIR CALLING
Weight of Words

When Mike Travis brought *El Gancho* to Publication Consultants, it was immediately clear the manuscript wasn't just historical fiction or a family memoir—it was a reckoning with the past, with identity, with legacy. Travis understood what many writers never quite grasp: writing carries more than words. It carries responsibility.

Set in the violent final years of Porfirio Díaz's regime in Mexico, *El Gancho* is a sweeping historical novel told with the intimacy of memory and the precision of someone who has sifted truth from family myth. It's the story of Prudenciano Nava, the writer's great-grandfather—a colleador, a rodeo star who became a refugee, a fugitive, a railroad worker, and ultimately, a man in exile from his own name.

Travis's commitment to truth—raw, uncomfortable, unsanitized—makes *El Gancho* endure. He doesn't mythologize Prudenciano. He paints him as a towering, reckless man, capable of both deep loyalty and devastating decisions. A man who kidnapped a child bride and later wept as typhoid stole one of his children. A man who caught bulls by their tails and drank too much tequila, who fought for his honor and fled for his life.

Travis wrote to understand. And in doing so, he gave voice to a generation of immigrants whose stories were buried beneath the rails they laid and the crops they picked. *El Gancho* is not simply about the Nava family. It's about every family crossing borders with more hope than belongings. Every man who made one bad choice too many, and every woman who followed him anyway.

But Mike reached past the borders of family history. He reached wider, capturing the overlooked intersection between the Mexican Revolution and American expansion. His prose reveals the hooks—*los ganchos*—drawing laborers north with promises of work and dignity, only to deliver hardship and anonymity. He wrote it because he believed readers deserved to remember the cost of the conveniences they now enjoy.

In a conversation about the book, Travis once said, "It's as if history is tapping us on the shoulder, asking us to take a good second look." This may be the clearest expression of what it means to write with responsibility. Not to lecture. Not to preach. But to tap, quietly but insistently, on the collective shoulder of memory.

There is no romanticizing here. No polish over pain. *El Gancho* doesn't ask you to admire Prudenciano Nava. It asks you to understand him. And in doing so, it invites readers to understand themselves—and the country they live in—just a little better.

Michael Travis could have left his family story to whispers and gravestones. Instead, he listened carefully to what history was saying. He shaped it into something lasting. And in the end, *El Gancho* does what the best writing always does: it changes the way we see what we thought we already knew.

This is what it means to carry the weight of words.

What makes Travis exceptional isn't just his ability to tell personal history. It's his willingness to step aside and let the story do the teaching.

Across all his books—from the family saga of *El Gancho* to the wilderness memoir *Melozi* to the civic history *The Landmen*—Travis shows writing is not about glorifying self. It's about honoring others—whether it's a flawed ancestor, a teenage version of yourself struggling to find footing in the bush, or the overlooked men who made modern Alaska possible.

Michael Travis wrote to remember. He wrote to illuminate. He wrote so the forgotten wouldn't stay forgotten.

This is the heart of responsible writing. And this is the legacy Travis is leaving behind.

Chapter Twelve: Writers Who Changed the World for the Better

QUIET IMPACT
When Words Heal

Bill Stokes wrote because his soul demanded it. After suffering profound personal loss, he found himself standing at the edge of grief—a place familiar to many but spoken of by few. In space, he chose not to escape or deny the pain. Instead, he wrote *Grieving—Hope—Joy*, a quiet book of poetry, becoming a lifeline not just for him, but for others walking through sorrow.

Bill understood something too many writers overlook: words don't need to be loud to be heard. They don't need to be polished to be powerful. When he sat down to write, he let his soul speak. In one recorded moment, without notes or rehearsal, he gave voice to something nearly unspeakable—the ache of longing, the cost of honesty, and the prayer of connection. "Could you trust me with your soul?" he asked. Not as a poet chasing accolades, but as a man offering his vulnerability.

This question—so simple, so raw—captured his entire approach to writing. For Bill, the responsibility of a writer wasn't just to rhyme sentences. It was to bleed truth. It was to trust somewhere, someone might find in his words the permission to grieve, to hope, and eventually, to rediscover joy. When he said, "There are things I can't say. God didn't give humans the ability to say what the soul knows. But the soul still tries," he named the quiet, sacred labor of writers who understand their calling.

The impact of Bill's work can't be measured in numbers. It lives instead in the tears of a single reader, the whispered "me too" of someone who thought they were alone. He understood the responsibility of writing—he carried it with reverence. His gift wasn't just putting feelings on paper. It was making others feel seen, without ever needing to say a word.

This is the kind of writer who changes the world—one soul at a time.

EVERYDAY HEROES

Shawn Lyons lived a meaningful life—and wrote about it. A classical guitarist, a literature professor, an ultramarathon runner, and a humble hiker who once climbed 12 peaks in 27.5 hours, Shawn was a Renaissance man by every definition except his own. He never claimed the title. He simply earned it.

His books, most notably the *Walk About Guide to Alaska* series, were not flashy productions. They were straightforward, deeply personal, and full of reverence for the land he loved. He wrote to invite others into the world he cherished—one trail, one story, one lesson at a time. Hikers across Alaska still tuck those books into their packs, trusting Shawn's directions like they'd trust a friend.

But the real power of his writing wasn't in the maps or the trail markers. It was in the spirit of the man himself. Shawn's quiet integrity was woven through every page. He rode his bike miles across town—even in the dead of winter—to pick up his own books. He'd stop to chat, share a laugh, then pedal home with 30 pounds strapped to his back like it was nothing. This grit—this gentleness—carried into his prose.

One afternoon, he asked for help recording a podcast. He wanted to share stories of hiking with his brother and father. We sat at my desk, I hit record, and he spoke. The episode was never broadcast. He passed away before he could record another. A single recording remains one of the most honest things I've ever heard—a man honoring the people and places shaping him.

Shawn gave people the desire to lace their boots and step outside. He taught his students to love words. He brought comfort through music and direction through maps. His books built a community.

If writing is about seeing the world more clearly, feeling less alone, or taking the next step with confidence, then Shawn Lyons succeeded beyond measure. He was an everyday writer. And his work still leads the way.

Challenge of Our Time

Writing in the Noise

Writers today are navigating a culture rewarding noise more than nuance. There's pressure to be fast, loud, and aligned with the moment's outrage, rather than grounded in something lasting. The challenge isn't just to

Chapter Twelve: Writers Who Changed the World for the Better

write—but to write with conscience in a time often confusing popularity with truth.

One of the growing tendencies I see is the dumbing down of writing—shortcuts in language, ideas without depth, and stories stripped of complexity for the sake of speed or trend. Social media hasn't helped. Too many writers mimic the tone of those platforms: loud, rude, and argumentative. This tone might catch attention, but it rarely earns respect—or changes hearts.

I'm also seeing writing with polite, politically correct words. Writers don't need to be offensive, but they do need to be honest. There's a difference between being polite and not speaking. And too many are playing it safe instead of saying something matters.

At Publication Consultants, I've always encouraged writers to write from their convictions, not from algorithms. But it's getting harder. Too many writers now ask what will sell before they ask what matters. The hardest part isn't shaping the story—it's having the strength to tell one few will understand. It takes grit to write what won't trend, patience to build something unlikely to go viral, and integrity to leave behind words you'd be proud to have read long after you're gone.

The world doesn't need more content. It needs more honesty. And today, takes more resolve than ever.

When everyone else is shouting, your quiet voice becomes the one people want to hear.

Where Hope Lives

Hope for meaningful writing doesn't come from trending hashtags or viral posts—it comes from quiet corners where readers still crave substance over spectacle. You see it in someone who underlines a passage and presses the book into a friend's hands. In the quiet dignity of librarians who know exactly where to find the story changes a life. In bookstore staff picks written in black marker and crooked script—"You'll love this if you've ever doubted and kept going."

It's in the writers who keep showing up to the page, not because they expect applause, but because they feel called to say something true. Writers who refuse to trade clarity for cleverness. Who won't flatten the complexity of life into slogans or soften the sharp edges of their message just to make it more marketable. They write with the confidence someone may need what they've written, even if someone doesn't come today.

And readers are still out there, too. Not always loud, not always easy to find, but present. Tired of noise, hungry for honesty, drawn to words holding weight.

Our world will always have trends. But meaning? Meaning is rooted. It's what endures long after the flash has faded. And where the hope is—in the steady, untrendy persistence of writing what matters. Hope lives in quiet corners where people still want substance over spectacle. You see hope when someone underlines something you wrote and passes it to a friend saying, 'You need to read this.' Such moments show your words matter.

Our Mission
Why I Do This Work

I have a saying: "Anyone fifty or older has a story to tell." And after more than forty years of publishing, I've found to be absolutely true. People carry stories needing to be preserved, stories about family, faith, work, war, love, loss, and the quiet victories never making the news. My job—our job at Publication Consultants—is to put those stories in print.

I don't just publish books. I publish the dreams of real people. Some want to pass down a legacy to their children. Others feel called to share something meant to uplift or heal someone else. And some just need to prove to themselves they can do it. Whether they want ten copies or ten thousand, I meet writers where they are. No other publisher offers the kind of flexibility I do—because I'm not chasing mass appeal; I'm honoring individual purpose.

What keeps me going isn't commercial success. It's seeing a first-time writer hold their book for the first time and say, "I didn't think I could do this." It's the quiet email from a reader who says, "This helped me." This is the reward. This is why I'm still here.

Chapter Twelve: Writers Who Changed the World for the Better

Ethics play a central role in everything I do. I've never wavered on this. I'm known for producing family-friendly books, and I don't include explicit content. This is a boundary I stand by—not to judge other publishers, but to keep my mission clear. When people publish with me, they know what I stand for. And trust matters.

This commitment to integrity is why I was honored with the Better Business Bureau's Torch Award—an acknowledgment of the values I've always held. At a time when many publishers are cutting corners, chasing trends, or selling shock, I've stayed true to what matters. My mission statement says it best: "I don't want to change the laws; I want to publish the books."

Publication Consultants isn't a corporation churning out pages for profit. I've walked the same road as the writers I serve. I understand the doubts, the rewrites, the joy of completion, and the vulnerability of letting their story go out into the world. I'm here to empower writers to act—and to act with purpose and skill.

This is why I still do this work. This is why I'll keep doing it. Because the world may be full of noise, but the right words still matter.

Whether you're writing books, family letters, workplace communications, or community newsletters, the mission remains the same: honor your audience, serve something larger than yourself, and use your words to make the world a little better than you found it.

THE LEGACY I CHOOSE

I'm not concerned about my legacy—the writer's legacy matters.

This is the truth of it. What's always mattered most to me is making sure writers—especially the ones who never thought they'd be called writer—get the chance to hold their own story in their hands. My role has been to equip people to tell the story only they can tell, and preserve it for the people who need to hear it.

Sometimes means ten copies for grandchildren. Sometimes it means thousands scattered across the world. Either way, the legacy belongs to the writer.

If people remember anything about Publication Consultants, I hope it's this: I never compromised my standards just to move faster or cheaper.

I stood beside writers with integrity. I honored their words. I did what I said I'd do.

And if they remember anything about me, I hope it's I believed words still change things—I spent my life empowering good people to say something lasting. Because they always had something worth saying. They just needed someone who believed they could say it.

This is the work. This is the mission. This is the legacy.

Your Invitation

Words Have Always Mattered

Words have always mattered. Yours still do.

You don't need to call yourself a writer to shape the world. If you write—anything—you're already part of the long tradition giving voice to what's most essential about us. Whether it's a letter to a friend, a note in a margin, a blog post, a sermon, a poem, a speech, or a book—writing takes heart. In a noisy, distracted, and divided world, this kind of heart is exactly what we need.

We created *The Power of Authors* because we believe in the enduring strength of meaningful writing. Not just publishing. Not just selling books. But writing with integrity and purpose—writing builds rather than breaks, connects rather than divides, and clarifies rather than confuses. We believe there's no small act when words are written with care.

What would we say if we could sit across from you right now? Simple. Your voice matters. Not because it's loud, but because it's yours. Because it carries your lived experience, your values, your insight, your sense of wonder, your heartbreak, your hope. No one else can offer. And someone—somewhere—needs it.

The world doesn't need more content. It needs more conviction.

You don't need to be a writer to write something meaningful. You don't need a platform to speak truth. But you do need to believe your voice is worth using. And if you're not sure of yet, let this be your proof: I believe it is.

Write. Speak. Share. Not because you're certain, but because you care. And when your words reach someone—and they will.

Chapter Twelve: Writers Who Changed the World for the Better

This is how the world changes. Not all at once. One word at a time.

You don't need to be published to be powerful. Every time you choose your words carefully and share them thoughtfully, you're already changing the world—one heart, one mind, one reader at a time.

You Already Have What Matters

You already write what matters—you just may not realize it yet.

A journal entry. A caption. A Facebook comment typed with trembling fingers. A text sent at just the right time. An email written to comfort, to ask forgiveness, to stand up, or to stand with.

This is not only about books. It never has been. It's about any words you write: carrying truth, kindness, memory, resistance, or hope. Writing is how we show our care. It's how we stand for something when we can't physically be there. It's how we say, *I see you,* when someone else feels invisible.

The world doesn't just need polished prose or bound volumes. It needs your voice—unedited and sincere. It needs words breaking through the flood of noise, not by volume, but by value. And value comes from being willing to speak what others only think.

You don't have to be published to be powerful. You don't have to be famous to be faithful to your truth. Whether you're writing a social post lifting someone's spirit or an email moving a team forward, you are shaping the emotional climate around you.

Don't wait until your words feel grand. Write them now—small, honest, human. This kind of writing doesn't shout for attention, but stays in someone's mind long after they've read it.

Because all writing matters when it's done with care. And your voice belongs in this world of words.

The Call Continues

Writers you've met in these pages—from Dickens to Dahl, from Achebe to Angelou—once faced the same blank page you face now. They wondered if their words would matter. They doubted their ability to reach anyone. They questioned whether the world needed another voice.

But they wrote anyway.

And because they did, lives changed. Nations awakened. Hearts healed. Hope spread. Truth endured.

Now it's your turn.

Not to write the next great American novel—though you might. Not to become famous—though fame may find you. But to take your place in the long line of those who believed words have power and used theirs for good.

The pen is still mightier than the sword. The story still changes the storyteller. And the right words, written at the right time, still have the power to change everything.

Your chapter is waiting to be written.

Begin.

Reflection: Answering the Call

The journey through these pages ends where it began—with you.

You've walked beside writers who faced wars and censorship, rejection and exile, loss and limitation. You've seen how words can awaken nations, defy silence, change reality, reflect humanity, and defend the invisible.

Now you know: every email you send, every letter you write, every post you share carries the same potential power.

The question isn't whether you're a writer. If you put words together with intention, you already are.

The question is: What will you do with this power?

Will you use your words to build up or tear down? To clarify or confuse? To connect or divide?

Writers in this book didn't wait for perfect circumstances or guaranteed audiences. They wrote because they had something worth saying—and they trusted their words would find their way to the people who needed them.

Your voice counts. Your story—told through whatever medium reaches your heart—can change someone's day, perspective, or life.

The torch has been passed to you.

What will you light with it?

Epilogue
The Journey Continues

As this book draws to a close, one truth rises above the rest: words are more than tools—they are vessels. Living things. Not merely carriers of information, but of influence. Not just thoughts on a page, but transformation in motion.

Throughout these pages, one thread has held steady. Authors—whether widely known or quietly working—carry a kind of quiet power. They bear witness. They ask better questions. They tell the truth as they see it. And in doing so, they offer us something more than insight—they offer the invitation to grow. A story told with honesty can soften walls. Even a question, if asked with humility, can open the door to healing.

What matters most here? What's the one thing to carry forward?

This: Every person who picks up a pen, taps a keyboard, or dares to speak into the world carries a measure of responsibility. Not to be flawless. Not to persuade every reader. But to try—to elevate rather than diminish, to clarify rather than confuse, and to bring light where others bring only noise.

Writing is not the gift of a chosen few. It is a calling available to anyone willing to use words with care and conviction. To speak truthfully. To listen humbly. And to believe language, when handled with sincerity, still has the power to heal, connect, and change things.

This is the quiet charge behind every chapter in this book: Use your words as if they matter—because they do.

The Power of Authors

YOU ARE PART OF THE STORY

When you finish this book, don't see yourself as an outsider looking in. You are part of the same enduring tradition. Authors we've discussed weren't born with guarantees. Most were ordinary people living ordinary lives—until they decided to pick up a pen and tell the truth as they saw it.

They didn't wait for permission. They didn't always know if their words would matter. Some never lived to see the impact of what they wrote. But the world changed because they wrote anyway.

This tradition continues. And you—yes, even if you're doubting, uncertain—have the power to join it. We recently spoke with one of our own authors, Halene Dahlstrom, who questioned whether her writing made any difference, despite having published several books. After reading her latest work, *Taramae: Return of the Ghost Girl*, I reminded her: her writing champions truth, even through fiction and fantasy. This makes her part of the tradition—no less than the historical authors we revere.

It's not about fame or sales. It's about standing for something. Every story, every poem, every paragraph written with conviction adds to the chain. You are not outside this tradition. You are already walking in its footsteps—now keep writing and leave some of your own.

Start where you are—grow where you're planted.

Robin Barefield didn't have high-speed internet, an MFA, or a big-city writing group. What she had was a generator, a remote outpost off Kodiak Island, and a dream. She showed up to an Alaska Writers Guild Conference years ago—older than most in the room, newer than many to writing—and handed me a manuscript she had poured herself into. This book became *Murder Over Kodiak*.

Robin didn't come to us with a platform or a publishing deal. She came with a story—and the heart to see it through.

Since then, she's written six novels, a nonfiction book, blogs, newsletters, is a charter member of Author Masterminds, and hosts two podcasts. She's accomplished this, not because she had an easy path, but because she believed she could grow into it. And she did.

When new writers feel overwhelmed by others' accomplishments, I remind them: every seasoned author once started with a blank page. Not one of them was born published. Every voice in this book had to take a first step—some barefoot, some late in life, and even one living on a remote island in Alaska.

You don't need to be ready. You need to be willing. You don't need to be known. You need to begin.

Your story doesn't have to be big to be worth telling. It just has to be yours.

SIMPLE POWER OF WORDS

If I could leave you with one image about the power of words, it would be a simple sentence—just seven words repeated ten times on a sheet of paper: *Mother said Richard the turtle is dead.*

No punctuation. No meaning.

For more than twenty years at the Young Writers Conference in the Matanuska Valley, our authors taught first through fifth graders what words can do. I handed out this sentence and asked each student (and parents and teachers) to punctuate it ten different ways. Every time, the room filled with laughter and surprise.

This one sentence—just seven plain words—could be shaped to say ten very different things. It could declare a pet's death. Or suggest Mother had killed someone. Or even hint *Mother* was the one who'd died.

Same words. Different power. All because of punctuation.

To me, this is the metaphor. Writing is made of pieces so small they can be dismissed—but they carry immense power when used with care. Without punctuation, a sentence is just noise. But with it, the noise becomes meaning. Purpose. Connection.

And this is what words do in the hands of a thoughtful writer. They move from random marks on a page to something shaping the reader—and sometimes, the world.

The image I leave you with isn't grand or poetic. It's a sheet of paper, a number two pencil, and seven words. A child discovering properly placed words can say many things.

This is why this work matters. And this is why it always will.

YOUR FIRST STEP

From time to time, I have the sacred responsibility of performing marriages in the temple. It's customary in those moments to pause and offer a word or two of counsel to the bride and groom—something simple, but lasting. I usually say something like this:

"Because marriage is a sacred ordinance—both a covenant and a contract—you'll feel something deep right now. The setting, the promises, the path bringing you here—it all combines into something you'll never quite feel again. So, before the moonlight and roses fade, write it down. Capture how you feel in this moment. Write it while it's fresh. You'll never be this close to the beginning again."

And then I tell them: "One day, when your children are grown and approaching their own marriage, you'll pull out the note—the one you wrote back then. You'll remember. You'll feel it all over again. And if you share it, they will see what's possible."

This is the same counsel I'd offer someone finishing this book.

Don't close the cover and walk away. Don't let the moment slip past unnoticed. Instead—write something. Even if it's just a line. Even if it's on a napkin, a receipt, the edge of a bulletin, the margin of the back page. What matters isn't where you write it. What matters is you write it.

You are not the same as you were before. This book has changed something in you—opened your eyes, stirred your spirit, anchored your voice. From now on, when you write, something will be different. You'll feel it in your hands. In your heart. You'll carry the weight of meaning with you. Every word will matter more. Every sentence will reach a little deeper. Because now you know what's at stake.

Just like the young couple kneeling at the altar, you're at the start of something new. Let it begin—not someday, not next week—but now.

Write what you're feeling. Write what matters.

Even just one sentence.

Because this book isn't a closing—it's an opening. A handoff. A quiet nudge toward your own voice.

Epilogue: The Journey Continues

We've told you stories. We've shown you the difference a sentence can make. Now it's your turn. Everyone writes. Grocery lists, job applications, emails, eulogies, notes on the fridge, texts saying "I'm sorry" or "I'm proud of you." Handwritten cards tucked into drawers and saved for years. Sermons, speeches, social media posts. Every word is a choice. Every sentence leaves a mark. You don't need a book deal to be a writer. You need only to recognize your words shape the world around you—quietly, steadily, and forever. Write with care, courage, and compassion.

WHERE HOPE LIVES

People want to read what matters. They want to write what matters. Even when the world feels loud and cluttered with noise, people are searching for quiet, clarity, and meaning. They want peace. They want progress. They want the kind of writing lifting, steadying, and strengthening them to face the challenges of their day.

Lasting stories aren't the loudest or the most sensational. They're the ones speaking to the soul. Stories about trials endured. Truth found. Hope restored. Scripture reminds us there is opposition in all things—but it also reminds us there's always a way through. The kind of writing helping people press forward with cheerful hearts—this is the writing readers remember. This is enduring writing.

Let's cut to the chase—vulgar or sensational writing might hit a list. But it fades. Writing lasting across decades—across generations—is the kind, speaking to the better part of us.

When I work with writers, I often say, "Don't get lost in the sideshow. Stay with the main event." Vulgar, discouraging, empty drama—this is a sideshow. The main event is what matters. What inspires, heals, strengthens, and restores. Stay there. This is where writing makes its mark.

And I have full confidence in readers of *The Power of Authors*. If they didn't know this when they opened the book, they know it now. It will change how they write and how they live.

This is where I see hope.

For Those Who Hesitate

To the hesitant reader wondering if there's anything worth saying, consider this: stories don't come from polish—they come from persistence.

Cil Gregoire, for instance. As a barefoot Cajun girl with wild dreams of Alaska, she built a log cabin, raised a family off the grid, homeschooled her son, and hauled water in the winter. During long winters, stories swirled in her head, and the grit to write one paragraph after another until a novel emerged—*Crystalline Aura*, followed by *Anthya's World*, *Elemental Forces*, *Interstellar Ruse*, and *Crystal Shards*.

Her journey wasn't easy. It took years. She wrote through the chores, through the seasons, and through self-doubt. And when the time came, she didn't ask, "Am I good enough?" She asked, "Where can I share this?" This is how she found Publication Consultants—and became an author others now look up to.

If you're hesitating, hear this: you don't need a perfect idea, a clear plan, or even a quiet house. You need to begin. You need to believe there's value in your lived experience—in the way you see the world, in the things only you can say.

Don't wait until life slows down or until the story's fully formed. Start now. And keep going. You'll be surprised how far a single sentence can take you.

Light Within

If these were the last words a reader encountered in this book, may they carry the quiet strength of someone like Author Masterminds member Rebecca Wetzler.

Rebecca has only published one book—*Bread Box for the Broken*—but she has lived many. Her life has walked through depression, chronic illness, and hardship with nothing more than steady faith and a willingness to speak gently from her scars. Raised in Alaska, shaped by solitude and shadow, Rebecca turned to Scripture not as a shield from suffering but as a light within it. Her devotional is not polished prose written from a mountaintop. It is bread handed out from the valley. And this makes it holy.

Epilogue: The Journey Continues

She often quotes John 8:12: *"Whoever follows me will never walk in darkness, but will have the light of life."* She writes from this glow, not from grand ambition. Her words remind us, authors don't need fame to matter. They need faith. They need honesty. They need to write when the lights go out, trusting the words will guide someone else home.

She never expected to become an editor, yet by quietly and patiently shaping their stories, she became one. Her kindness with fellow authors and careful eye for truth in sentence and soul have made her a cornerstone among Author Masterminds members—not because she sought recognition, but because she served.

If you're reading these final lines still wondering whether your story counts, remember this: Rebecca wrote to help. She didn't wait for the storm to pass. She wrote in the rain. And in doing so, she lit a path for others.

Follow her lead. Share your truth. Let your story speak—even if your voice trembles. What you've lived may be the very words someone else needs to keep going.

This is the power of authors.

The journey doesn't end here. It begins again tomorrow, in the first word you choose to write.

—Evan and Lois Swensen

INDEX

A

Achebe, Chinua, 32-33
  Things Fall Apart, 32
AI (Artificial Intelligence)
  Statement about use in book, 3
  In publishing and research, 117
Alaska
  Authors and settings, 5-6, 8, 15, 42-43, 55-56, 64-65, 92-93, 96-98, 106-107, 120-121, 128-129, 137-139
  Every Reason You Should Leave Alaska, 106-107
  Gardening Guide, 138
  Outdoors Radio Magazine, 23
  Writers and themes, 15, 33-34
Alcott, Louisa May, 19-20
  Little Women, 20
Anderson, Andy , 70-71
  Alaska Bush Cop, 70-71
Angelou, Maya, 27
Arnett, Betty, 74
  22 and the Mother of 11, 74
Atamian, Sarkis, 139
  The Bears of Manley, 139
Austen, Jane, 54
  Pride and Prejudice, 54

Authors
  Defending the invisible, 91-101
  Enduring legacy of, 127-141
  Everyday writers, quiet strength of, 103-112
  Power and responsibility of, 144, 157
  Who changed the world for better, 143-156
  Who defied silence, 27-37

B

Bache-Wiig, Denny, 81
  Nothing Ventured, 81
Bacon, Francis, 103
Baker, Eva (with Martha Maiwald), 107-108
  Martha and Eva, 107-108
Barefield, Robin, 158
  Murder Over Kodiak, 158
Barske, Dianne, 95
  Mostly Music, 95
Bassette, Suzanne, 145-147
  Talkeetna Twines, 145-147
Becker, Nancy, 15
  Trapline Chatter, 15
Better Business Bureau Torch Award, 123, 153

INDEX

Boylan, Jan (with Dolores Roguszka), 136-137
  The Day Trees Bent to the Ground, 136-137
Bridges, LaVon (with Alice Wright), 108-109
  Alaska Animals, We Love You!, 108-109
Browning, Elizabeth Barrett, 60-61
Buck, Pearl S., 41-42
  The Good Earth, 41
Bulwer-Lytton, Edward, 17

C

Calvino, Italo, 120
Cameron, Marc (formerly Marc Otte), 104
  Pray for Justice, 104
  Hide and Seek, 104
Camus, Albert, 39
Cather, Willa, 42-43
  My Ántonia, 42
  O Pioneers!, 42
Characters
  Creating believable, 104-105
  Inner landscape of, 104
  Who feel real, 131-132
Christie, Agatha, 84-86
Conkle, Lenora, 5-6, 8
  Hunting the Way It Was in Our Changing Alaska, 5-6, 8
Conklin, Marissa, 91
  It Happens Here Too, 91
Cook, Richard (illustrator), 79
Cox, Bill, 118
  My Pursuit of the Axis of Evil, 118
Crosby, Ruthann, 79-80
  Miracle in the Glass, 79-80
Currier, Frederick James, 55
  An Alaskan Adventure, 55

D

Dahl, Roald, 107-108

Dahlstrom, Halene, 158
  Taramae: Return of the Ghost Girl, 158
Dahlstrom, Kati, 34-35
  Turtle in a Racehorse World, 34-35
de Mille, Agnes, 59
Dickens, Charles, 18-19
  Nicholas Nickleby, 18
  Oliver Twist, 18
Dickinson, Emily, 52
Digital tools and timeless truths, 113-125
Dillingham, Mike, 130-131
  Rivers: Diary of a Blind Alaska Racing Sled Dog, 130
Donne, John, 91
Donkersloot, Sara, 64-65, 128-129
  Down by the River, 64, 128
  Out on the Tundra, 128
Douglass, Carl, 19
  The Last Phoenix, 19
Doyle, Sir Arthur Conan, 105
  Sherlock Holmes stories, 105

E

eBooks, 114-115
Eliot, George, 53
  Middlemarch, 53
Eliot, T.S., 51
Endurance, elements of, 111
Evanson, Jane L. PhD, 5-6
  Writer, Editor, Speaker, and Trainer, 5-6

F

Ferber, Edna, 131-132
  Giant, 131
  So Big, 131
Fiction
  Changing reality, 39-49
  Creating through community, 135-137
  Responsibility in writing, 47-48
  Warning through imagination, 44-46

INDEX

Fields, Weston, 133-134
The Dead Sea Scrolls: A Full History, 133-134
Flint, Mary, 62-63
Red Star, 62-63
Frank, Anne, 29-30
Franklin, Benjamin, 20-21
Poor Richard's Almanack, 21
Freestone, Adam, 60-61

G

Gebb, Sheldon, 53, 85
In the Footsteps of My Father, 53, 85
Golding, William, 43-44
Lord of the Flies, 43-44
Goodman, Lilly, 97-98
Candle Sparks, 97-98
Gregoire, Cil, 162
Crystalline Aura, 162
Anthya's World, 162

H

Hardy, Thomas, 54-55
Hardesty, Victoria (with Nancy Perez), 121-122
Wonder Horse series, 121-122
Harmer, Mike, 68-69
How To Go Blind and Not Lose Your Mind, 68-69
Harrison, Lorene Cuthbertson, 95
Havel, Václav, 127
Hawthorne, Nathaniel, 93-94, 143
The Scarlet Letter, 93
Quote
Hemingway, Ernest, 67, 71-72
Hersh, Seymour, 116-118
Hills, Dolly, 72
A Mother's Tears for a Missing Son, 72
Holeman, Maggie, 31-32
Woman in the Locker Room, 32

Homme, Joseph, 73
Cures and Chaos, 6, 73
Hootch, Molly, 33
Molly Hootch: I Remember When, 33
Hope
In writing and literature, 151-152, 161
Where it lives, 161
Hugo, Victor, 30-31
Hunt, Kayla, 44
Caged Eagles, 44
Hunt, Ollen, 8
Buffalo Soldier: What My Country Did for Me—What I Did for My Country, 8

I-J

Imagination and storytelling, 44-46
Integrity in writing, 144-145, 147, 152-153
Jacobson, Anna, 96-97
Elnguq, 96-97
Jacobson, Jake, 118-119
James, Henry, 104
Johnson, Dr. Matthew, 56
Positive Parenting with a Plan, 56

L

L'Engle, Madeleine, 128
A Wrinkle in Time, 128
Larsen, Courtney, 144-145
Lee, Harper, 40-41
To Kill a Mockingbird, 40-41
Legacy
Creating lasting, 127-141
Of writers, 153-154
Lehe, Heather, 55-56
Colony Kids, 55-56
Levi, Steve, 46-47
The Matter of Gift Mortgages, 46-47

Index

Lewis, C.S., 28-29
   The Lion, the Witch, and the Wardrobe, 28
   The Poison of Subjectivism, 28
Lloyd, Gita (illustrator), 105-106
Lyons, Shawn, 149-150
   Walk About Guide to Alaska series, 150

M

MacDonald, George, 95
   The Princess and the Goblin, 95
Maiwald, Martha (with Eva Baker), 107-108
   Martha and Eva, 107-108
Mandela, Nelson, 77
Mansfield, Katherine, 69-70
   Bliss, 69
   The Garden Party, 69
   Miss Brill, 69
Martin, Elizabeth and Merle, 94
   I'm Just Her Father, 94
Masek, Beverly (Representative), 23
Matthews, Bonnye, 63-64
   Ki'ti's Story, 75,000 BC, 63
   Winds of Change series, 63
McLuhan, Marshall, 113
Melville, Herman, 82
   Billy Budd, 82
   Moby-Dick, 82
Miller, Darlene, 45
   Surviving Disasters and Finding Grace, 45
Milne, A.A., 106-107
   Charlotte's Web, 106
Montgomery, L.M., 55-56
   Anne of Green Gables, 55
Moral responsibility in writing, 16, 24, 144
Munro, Alice, 114
Mystrom, Rick, 87-88
   My Wonderful Life with Diabetes, 88
   Glucose Control Eating, 88
   What Should I Eat?, 88
   Your Type 2 Diabetes Lifeline, 88

N-O

Narrative authority, 32-33
O'Neil, T. Martin, 30, 36
   Into the Fire, 30
Ogan, Scott (Representative), 23-24
Orwell, George, 21-22
   1984, 21-22
   Animal Farm, 21
Otte, Marc (see Cameron, Marc), 104

P

Perez, Nancy (with Victoria Hardesty), 121-122
   Wonder Horse series, 121-122
Persistence in writing, 77-89
Poll, Mary Ann, 119-120
   Real Ghost Chatter podcast, 119
Potter, Beatrix, 80-81
   The Tale of Peter Rabbit, 80
Preston, Dale (illustrator), 64, 128
Prewitt, Frank, 22
   Last Bridge to Nowhere, 22
Proust, Marcel, 134-135
   In Search of Lost Time, 134
Publication Consultants
   Mission and values, 152-153
   Worldwide Distribution Service, 116

Q-R

Quiet Echo, 47
   Collaborative novel, 47
Quiet strength of everyday writers, 103-112
Readers and Writers Book Club, 119, 124
Responsibility of writers, 144, 157
Ritter, Rich, 43
   Heart of Abigail, 43

Roberts, Ann D., 138
  Alaska Gardening Guide, 138
Roguszka, Dolores (with Janet Boylan), 136-137
  The Day Trees Bent to the Ground, 136-137
Rowling, J.K., 79-80
  Harry Potter and the Philosopher's Stone, 79

S

Sacks, Oliver, 83-84
  An Anthropologist on Mars, 84
  Awakenings, 84
  The Man Who Mistook His Wife for a Hat, 84
Schlegelmilch, Marianne, 131-132
  Acts of Kindness, 131
  Feather from a Stranger, 131
Schuldt, Dwaine, 137-138
  Lt. Henry Tureman Allen expedition journal, 137-138
Shaginoff, Ingrid, 92-93
  Alaskan wilderness memoir, 92-93
Shakespeare, William, 135-137
Shelley, Mary, 44-45
  Frankenstein, 44-45
Simpson, Ron, 42
  Legacy of the Chief, 42
Singer, Isaac Bashevis, 92-93
Smith-Phillips, Fran, 72
  The Search for Dale's Plane, 72
Social change through writing, 18-24
Stevenson, Robert Louis, 121
  Dr. Jekyll and Mr. Hyde, 121
  Economy as literary virtue, 121
Stokes, Bill, 149
  Grieving—Hope—Joy, 149
Storytelling
  Digital-age, 120-122
  Power of, 47-48, 159
  Responsibility in, 47-48

Swensen, Evan, 7-9, 157, 163
  Co-author of *The Power of Authors*
  Publisher at Publication Consultants
Swensen, Lois, 7-9, 163
  Co-author of *The Power of Authors*
  Alaska Outdoors Radio Magazine, 23
Szymborska, Wislawa, 97-98
  Cat in an Empty Apartment, 97

T

Taylor, Robin (Senator), 23-24
Thomas, Kirk, 105-106
  Grandpa's Airplane, 105-106
Thoreau, Henry David, 83
  Civil Disobedience, 83
  Walden, 83
Tolkien, J.R.R., 110
Tolstoy, Leo, 22-23
  Anna Karenina, 23
  War and Peace, 23
Travis, Mike, 147-148
  El Gancho, 147-148
  Melozi, 148
  The Landmen, 148
Trollope, Anthony, 118-119
Troy, Warren, 138-139
  Mike in the Woods, 138-139
Truth
  As foundation for writing, 132-134
  Telling difficult truths, 107-108
  Through fiction, 39-49
Twain, Mark, 70
  Adventures of Huckleberry Finn, 70

U-V

Updike, John, 115-116
Vaccaro, Gasper (illustrator), 105-106
Verhagen, Josh, 120-121
  Eddie the Ermine, 120-121
Verne, Jules, 98-99

W

Wamatu, John Nganga, 98-99
  A Blessed Journey, 99
Wells, H.G., 46
  The Island of Dr. Moreau, 46
  The Time Machine, 46
  The War of the Worlds, 46
Wetzler, Rebecca, 162-163
  Bread Box for the Broken, 162
Wharton, Edith, 78
  The Age of Innocence, 78
  The House of Mirth, 78
White, E.B., 96-97
  Charlotte's Web, 96
Wilder, Laura Ingalls, 61-62
  Little House in the Big Woods, 61
Winans, Valerie, 54
  The Extraordinary Life of Edwin B. Winans, 54
Wood, Dr. Deb, 134-135
  The Truth About Suicide, 134-135
Wordsworth, William, 68
  Lyrical Ballads, 68
Wright, Alice (with LaVon Bridges), 108-109
  Alaska Animals, We Love You!, 108-109
Wright, Richard, 31-32
  Native Son, 31

Writers
  As builders of better world, 13-16
  Awakening nations through words, 17-25
  Digital tools and timeless truths, 113-125
  Moral responsibility of, 144, 157
  Power and calling of, 1-12
  Who defended the invisible, 91-101
  Who paid the price, 67-75
Writing
  As sacred responsibility, 144
  Digital challenges in, 116-118
  For unknown readers, 128-131
  Impact and significance of, 145-147
  In noisy environments, 116-118
  Integrity in, 144-145, 147
  Quiet strength in, 103-112
  Sustainable production in, 118-120

Y-Z

Yeats, W.B., 129-131
Young Writers Conference, 159
Zola, Émile, 132-133
  J'Accuse...!, 132
  Rougon-Macquart cycle, 132

www.ingramcontent.com/pod-product-compliance
Lightning Source LLC
Chambersburg PA
CBHW070804100426
42742CB00012B/2241